WILLIAMS-SONOMA

ROASTING

RECIPES AND TEXT
BARBARA GRUNES

GENERAL EDITOR
CHUCK WILLIAMS

PHOTOGRAPHS
MAREN CARUSO

SIMON & SCHUSTER • **SOURCE**

NEW YORK • LONDON • TORONTO • SYDNEY • SINGAPORE

CONTENTS

THE CLASSICS

POULTRY

BEEF, VEAL, AND VENISON

PORK AND LAMB

FISH AND SHELLFISH

VEGETABLES AND FRUITS

INTRODUCTION

Roasting is one of our oldest and most traditional forms of cooking. Whether it's a leg of lamb, a whole chicken, or asparagus, the time these foods spend roasting in the oven yields tender juicy interiors and rich caramelized exteriors that no other cooking method can rival. And because roasting is so simple—often all it takes is simple seasoning and then waiting for the delicious results—it need not be limited to holidays or special occasions. Try roasting a beef tenderloin or pork chops for a weeknight dinner or potatoes and other vegetables for an easy side dish. Even apples or plums can be roasted for a simple but succulent dessert.

Throughout this cookbook, each recipe is paired with a side note that highlights a particular ingredient or technique. In addition, a chapter of basics tells you all you need to begin roasting, including information on equipment, preparing, timing, and carving. I hope the tempting recipes inside will inspire you to make roasting a regular part of your weekday as well as weekend cooking.

Chuck Williams

THE CLASSICS

The roasting recipes in this chapter can play important roles in a cook's basic repertoire. Beef tenderloin sliced and served with roasted mushrooms is a perfect Sunday dinner, while turkey brushed with a glistening currant glaze brightens a Thanksgiving table. Or, a simple side dish of roasted potatoes or peppers can round out a myriad of menus with minimal effort.

CHICKEN WITH HERB STUFFING

To make the stuffing, preheat the oven to 350°F (180°C). Arrange the bread cubes in a single layer on a baking sheet, put in the oven, and bake, turning twice, until golden, about 15 minutes. Set aside. In a large frying pan over medium heat, melt the butter. Add the chopped onion and sauté until translucent, about 5 minutes. Remove from the heat and add the bread cubes, parsley, sage, and salt and pepper to taste. Toss to mix. Set aside.

Raise the oven temperature to 400°F (200°C). Rinse the chicken under cold running water, discarding the giblets, and pat dry. Remove and discard any loose fat. Starting from the neck end, use your fingers to loosen the skin over the breast without piercing it. Slide the sage leaves under the skin. Brush the chicken with the melted butter and season inside and out with salt and pepper. Stuff the chicken with the bread cubes, and truss if desired (page 106). Place the chicken, breast side up, in an oiled flameproof roasting pan just large enough to hold it comfortably and add the onion.

Roast the chicken until the leg joints move easily and the juices run clear when a thigh is pierced with a knife, 1–1¼ hours. An instant-read thermometer inserted into the thickest part of the thigh (but not touching bone) should read 170°F (77°C).

Transfer the chicken to a carving board, cover loosely with aluminum foil, and let rest for 10 minutes. Meanwhile, place the pan over medium-high heat and skim off the surface fat. Add the stock and deglaze the pan, stirring with a wooden spoon to scrape up the browned bits. Bring to a boil and cook until reduced by half, about 4 minutes. In a food processor or blender, purée the pan sauce and onion. Season with salt and pepper.

Carve the chicken (page 109) and arrange on a warmed platter. Top with the sauce. Serve the stuffing alongside.

MAKES 5–6 SERVINGS

DEGLAZING

Deglazing is a French technique used to make sauces from pan juices. To deglaze a pan, remove the poultry or meat that was cooked in it and skim off any surface fat, leaving behind the drippings and browned bits. Place the pan over medium-high heat and pour stock or another liquid such as water or wine into the hot pan. As the liquid boils, use a wooden spoon to stir and scrape up the browned bits from the bottom of the pan. These roasted tidbits give rich flavor to the stock, which thickens into a sauce as you let the liquid partly boil away, or reduce.

FOR THE HERB STUFFING:

2–2½ cups (4–5 oz/ 125–155 g) trimmed white bread cubes

4 tablespoons (2 oz/60 g) unsalted butter

1 yellow onion, chopped

½ cup (¾ oz/20 g) finely chopped fresh flat-leaf (Italian) parsley

2 teaspoons finely chopped fresh sage or 1 teaspoon dried

Salt and freshly ground pepper

1 roasting chicken, 4½–5½ lb (2.25–2.75 kg)

5 fresh sage leaves

2 tablespoons unsalted butter, melted

Salt and freshly ground pepper

1 large yellow onion, thickly sliced

¾ cup (6 fl oz/180 ml) chicken stock (page 110) or canned low-sodium broth

LEG OF LAMB WITH ROASTED GARLIC

1 boneless leg of lamb,
4–4½ lb (2–2.25 kg)

8 large heads garlic, plus
2 large cloves

Olive oil for coating

2 teaspoons finely
chopped fresh rosemary
or 1 teaspoon dried

1 teaspoon finely
chopped fresh thyme
or ½ teaspoon dried

Place an oven rack in the lower third of the oven and preheat to 425°F (220°C). Trim the lamb of any loose fat. Open the lamb roast flat, cut side down, and tuck any thin pieces under to make a roast of uniform thickness. Place the lamb in an oiled heavy roasting pan just large enough to hold it comfortably. Peel the 2 garlic cloves and cut into a total of 10 slivers. Make 10 small cuts in the lamb and insert a garlic sliver in each. Coat the lamb with olive oil and sprinkle with the rosemary and thyme.

Roast the lamb for 15 minutes. Reduce the heat to 350°F (180°C) and continue roasting until an instant-read thermometer inserted into the thickest part of the lamb reads 125°F (52°C) for rare, about 1½ hours.

Meanwhile, remove the outermost papery layer of skin from the 8 garlic heads and cut off the top of each head to expose the cloves. Coat the heads with olive oil and wrap each head individually in aluminum foil. Arrange the heads, cut side up, in a baking dish. Put the garlic in the oven 40–50 minutes before the lamb is due to be done, and roast until very soft when pressed.

Transfer the lamb to a carving board, cover loosely with aluminum foil, and let stand for 5–10 minutes. Slice the lamb across the grain and arrange on a warmed platter. Skim the surface fat from the pan juices and spoon the juices over the lamb. Unwrap the garlic heads and discard the foil. Serve the lamb with the roasted garlic alongside for each diner to spread on the lamb.

MAKES 8 SERVINGS

ROASTED GARLIC

Roasting tames garlic's pungency and brings out its sweetness. To use roasted garlic, simply squeeze each clove so that the soft pulp slips out of its skin. Roasted garlic may be served as an appetizer, spread on pieces of coarse country bread or slices of toast.

BEEF TENDERLOIN WITH MUSHROOMS

Preheat the oven to 400°F (200°C). Trim the tenderloin of any loose fat and discard. Place the roast in an oiled roasting pan just large enough to hold it comfortably. Coat the meat with 1–2 tablespoons of the melted butter and sprinkle with the thyme, sage, and salt and pepper to taste.

In a bowl, mix the remaining 4 tablespoons (2 oz/60 g) melted butter and the garlic. Toss the mushrooms with the flavored butter and add them to the roasting pan.

Roast the tenderloin and mushrooms, basting the meat with the pan drippings and turning the mushrooms twice, until an instant-read thermometer inserted into the center of the roast reads 130°F (54°C) for medium-rare, about 1 hour and 20 minutes.

Transfer the tenderloin to a carving board, cover loosely with aluminum foil, and let stand for 10 minutes. Slice the beef across the grain and arrange on a warmed platter, surrounded with the roasted mushrooms. Skim the surface fat from the pan juices and spoon the juices over all.

MAKES 8 SERVINGS

WILD MUSHROOM VARIATION

A wide variety of mushrooms is available these days. Most are not truly harvested from the wild but, like white button mushrooms, are cultivated. Try replacing some or all of the white mushrooms in this recipe with brown cremini (baby portobellos), meaty shiitakes, or oyster mushrooms. If you can find them in the market, use true wild mushrooms such as chanterelles, porcini (also known as ceps), or morels, which have an outstanding woodsy flavor.

1 beef tenderloin roast (short loin), 3½–4 lb (1.75–2 kg)

5–6 tablespoons (2½–3 oz/ 75–90 g) unsalted butter, melted

1 teaspoon finely chopped fresh thyme or ½ teaspoon dried

1 teaspoon finely chopped fresh sage or ½ teaspoon dried

Salt and freshly ground pepper

1 teaspoon minced garlic

2 lb (1 kg) fresh white button mushrooms, brushed clean and thickly sliced

TURKEY WITH CURRANT GLAZE

FOR THE CURRANT GLAZE:

¾ cup (7½ oz/235 g)
red currant jam

¼ cup (2 fl oz/60 ml) dry
red wine

2 tablespoons Dijon
mustard

1 clove garlic, minced

1 turkey, 10–12 lb (5–6 kg)

2–3 tablespoons unsalted
butter, melted

To make the glaze, combine the jam, wine, mustard, and garlic in a small saucepan. Cook over medium heat, stirring, until the jam has melted and the ingredients are blended. Remove from the heat and let cool.

Place an oven rack in the lower third of the oven and preheat to 400°F (200°C). Rinse the turkey under cold running water and remove and discard the giblets, any loose fat, and the tail. Pat dry with paper towels. Place the turkey, breast side down, in an oiled heavy roasting pan just large enough to hold it comfortably.

Roast the turkey for 30 minutes, then reduce the oven temperature to 325°F (165°C). Remove the turkey from the oven, turn it breast side up, and brush with the melted butter. Return it to the oven and continue roasting, brushing the turkey with the glaze 2 times during the last hour of roasting, until the leg joints move easily and the juices run clear when a thigh is pierced with a knife, about 2 hours. An instant-read thermometer inserted into the thickest part of the thigh (but not touching bone) should read 175°F (80°C).

Transfer the turkey to a carving board, cover loosely with aluminum foil, and let stand for 10 minutes. Carve the turkey (page 109), arrange on a warmed platter, and serve.

Serving Tip: Serve the bird surrounded by roasted autumn vegetables (page 99). Use the pan drippings for making basic gravy (page 110).

MAKES 10–12 SERVINGS

RED CURRANTS

The bright scarlet color and refreshingly tart flavor of these berries make them a good foil for meats and poultry. They also have a high level of pectin, a natural jelling agent, that makes them an ideal fruit for turning into sauces, jellies, and jams. Clusters of the small round berries can be found in many farmers' markets during summer, while the more widely available red currant jams and jellies are available at specialty-food stores and well-stocked supermarkets.

SALMON WITH TARRAGON BUTTER

To make the tarragon butter, in a food processor, combine the butter, tarragon leaves, vinegar, and salt and pepper to taste. Process for a few seconds, just until the ingredients are combined. Spoon into a small bowl and cover, or form into a log in waxed paper. Refrigerate for at least 30 minutes or for up to 3 days. Bring to cool room temperature before serving.

Preheat the oven to 450°F (230°C). Put the salmon in an oiled roasting pan just large enough to hold it comfortably. Coat the fish with olive oil and season it inside and out with salt and pepper. Put the tarragon sprigs inside the fish.

In a bowl, toss together the tomatoes and onion. Sprinkle the tomato mixture over the salmon.

Roast the salmon until juices begin to collect in the roasting pan and the flesh flakes easily when gently prodded with a fork, 20–25 minutes.

Remove the salmon from the oven and let stand for 10 minutes. Using 2 spatulas, carefully transfer the salmon to a warmed platter and surround it with the tomato mixture. To serve, peel back the skin if desired and cut the fish crosswise. Top the individual servings with pats of tarragon butter.

MAKES 6-8 SERVINGS

PEELING TOMATOES

Peeling eliminates the shreds of skin that result when you cook fresh tomatoes—bits unpleasant to both the eye and the palate. To peel tomatoes, cut a shallow X in the bottom end of each one and drop them, a few at a time, into boiling water for 15–30 seconds (depending on ripeness) to loosen the skin. Using a slotted spoon, transfer to a bowl of ice water to stop the cooking. When cool enough to handle, use your fingers to pull off the skin. To seed the tomatoes, halve them crosswise and gently squeeze out the seeds and the juice. Cut out the core and proceed with the recipe.

FOR THE TARRAGON BUTTER:

½ cup (4 oz/125 g) unsalted butter, cut into tablespoon-sized pieces, at room temperature

2 tablespoons fresh tarragon leaves

2 tablespoons red wine vinegar

Salt and freshly ground pepper

1 whole salmon, 4–5 lb (2–2.5 kg), cleaned and head removed

Olive oil for coating

Salt and freshly ground pepper

4 fresh tarragon sprigs

2 tomatoes, peeled and seeded *(far left)*, then chopped (about 1½ cups/9 oz/280 g)

1 small yellow onion, chopped

ROASTED NEW POTATOES

1 lb (500 g) small to medium new potatoes, scrubbed

¼ cup (2 fl oz/60 ml) extra-virgin olive oil

1 tablespoon finely chopped fresh rosemary or 1½ teaspoons dried

3 cloves garlic, minced

Salt and freshly ground pepper

Preheat the oven to 450°F (230°C). In a large bowl, toss the potatoes with the ¼ cup olive oil, rosemary, garlic, and salt and pepper to taste.

Arrange the potatoes in a single layer on an oiled baking sheet or roasting pan. Roast, stirring and turning occasionally, until fork-tender, 45–55 minutes; the timing will depend on the size of the potatoes.

Transfer the potatoes to a warmed serving dish and serve at once.

MAKES 6 SERVINGS

NEW POTATOES

These young tubers, found in farmers' markets and green-grocers in spring and early summer, are freshly dug immature waxy potatoes. The red ones are the most common, but other varieties may be found. New potatoes are thin-skinned and must be used soon after harvest. True new potatoes are available for only a short time each year, but any small, thin-skinned waxy potato, such as red or white creamers or fingerlings, may be used instead.

ROASTED BELL PEPPERS

Preheat the oven to 475°F (245°C). Put the bell peppers on a baking sheet and roast, turning several times to cook evenly, until charred and blistered all over, 15–20 minutes.

Transfer the peppers to a paper bag. Close the bag and let the peppers steam until cool to the touch, 10–15 minutes. Rub and pull off the charred skin. Slice each pepper in half lengthwise and discard the seeds, ribs, and stems. Cut the peppers lengthwise into narrow strips and put in a shallow bowl.

In a small bowl, whisk together the olive oil, vinegar, garlic, oregano, and salt and pepper to taste. Drizzle the dressing over the peppers and sprinkle with the capers. Toss. Let stand at room temperature for 30 minutes, or cover and refrigerate for up to 24 hours. Bring the peppers to room temperature before serving.

Line a platter with the arugula. Arrange the peppers on top of the arugula and serve.

MAKES 6 SERVINGS

BELL PEPPER VARIETIES

Bell peppers (capsicums) come in a range of colors, and their flavor varies accordingly. The common green bell pepper is unripe and tart. As it matures, it turns red and grows sweeter. Other colored peppers, such as yellow and orange or even purple or brown, are separate varieties. If you prefer sweeter bell peppers, replace the green pepper in this recipe with a yellow or orange one. Bell peppers are a pretty addition to the home vegetable garden. When you have a bumper crop, roast and freeze them to use in sauces, salads, or soups or as a garnish.

1 large green bell pepper (capsicum)

1 large red bell pepper (capsicum)

1 large yellow bell pepper (capsicum)

¼ cup (2 fl oz/60 ml) extra-virgin olive oil

3 tablespoons balsamic vinegar

2 cloves garlic, minced

1 teaspoon minced fresh oregano or ½ teaspoon dried

Salt and freshly ground pepper

1 tablespoon capers

1 bunch arugula (rocket), stemmed

POULTRY

Bringing a crisp and evenly browned roasted bird with a tender, succulent interior to the dinner table will make any cook proud. Whether it's a holiday goose, an Asian-style duck, or a chicken that yields enough leftover meat for meals on busy weeknights, roasted poultry is a universally appealing comfort food.

CHICKEN WITH LEMON AND ONION
26

CAPON WITH MANGO GLAZE
29

CHICKEN WITH CHILE AND LIME
30

CORNISH HENS PROVENÇAL
33

TURKEY BREAST WITH ROASTED PEARS
34

CHINESE-STYLE DUCK
37

GOOSE WITH ROASTED APPLES
38

CHICKEN WITH LEMON AND ONION

Preheat the oven to 400°F (200°C). Rinse the chicken under cold running water, discarding the giblets, and pat dry with paper towels. Remove and discard any loose fat. Place the chicken, breast side up, in an oiled heavy roasting pan just large enough to hold it comfortably. Coat the chicken with olive oil and drizzle with the lemon juice. Sprinkle the chicken inside and out with the oregano and salt and pepper. Arrange the onion slices around the chicken and place the lemon slices over the chicken. Brush the onions and lemon slices with olive oil.

Roast the chicken until the leg joints move easily and the juices run clear when a thigh is pierced with a knife, 1–1¼ hours. An instant-read thermometer inserted into the thickest part of the thigh (but not touching bone) should read 170°F (77°C). Turn the onions once during roasting.

Transfer the chicken to a carving board, cover loosely with aluminum foil, and let stand for 10 minutes. Carve the chicken (page 109) and arrange on a warmed platter. Garnish with parsley and serve, with the onions and lemon if desired.

Serving Tip: Use the pan drippings from this recipe for making basic gravy (page 110).

MAKES 5–6 SERVINGS

**1 roasting chicken,
4½–5½ lb (2.25–2.75 kg)**

Olive oil for coating

**¼ cup (2 fl oz/60 ml) fresh
lemon juice**

**4 teaspoons minced fresh
oregano or 2 teaspoons
dried**

**Salt and freshly ground
pepper**

**2 large red onions, thickly
sliced**

**1 lemon, sliced into rounds
¼ inch (6 mm) thick**

**Chopped fresh flat-leaf
(Italian) parsley for garnish**

TRUSSING

Chicken and other birds are sometimes trussed, or tied into a neat, compact shape for cooking. This is done for aesthetic reasons; the bird may actually cook more evenly if it is left untrussed. If you wish to truss, tuck the wing tips underneath the breasts, to keep them from singeing, then cross the drumsticks and tie them together with linen kitchen string. Meat may also be trussed for roasting, but in that case the trussing is done to ensure more even cooking.

CAPON WITH MANGO GLAZE

FOR THE MANGO GLAZE:

2 ripe mangoes, cubed (far right)

1 cup (8 fl oz / 150 ml) mango juice (see Notes)

1 capon, 6–7 lb (3–3.5 kg) (see Notes)

Canola oil for coating

Salt and freshly ground pepper

Toasted sliced almonds for garnish

1 ripe mango, diced

To make the mango glaze, combine the mango cubes and juice in a food processor or blender and purée. Pour the purée into a small bowl and set aside.

Preheat the oven to 400°F (200°C). Rinse the capon under cold running water, discarding the giblets, and pat the bird dry with paper towels. Remove and discard any loose fat. Cut off the wing tips and tail. Place the capon, breast side up, in an oiled roasting pan just large enough to hold it comfortably. Coat the outside of the capon with canola oil. Season inside and out with salt and pepper.

Roast the capon until the leg joints move easily and the juices run clear when a thigh is pierced with a knife, 2¼–2¾ hours. An instant-read thermometer inserted into the thickest part of the thigh (but not touching bone) should read 170°F (77°C). Brush the capon with mango glaze 30 minutes before the end of the roasting time, and again 15 minutes later.

Transfer the capon to a carving board, cover loosely with aluminum foil, and let stand for 10 minutes. Meanwhile, in a small saucepan over medium heat, bring the remaining mango glaze to a boil for 1 minute.

Carve the capon (page 109) and arrange on a warmed platter. Garnish with the almonds and diced mango. Serve the remaining glaze alongside as a sauce.

Notes: A capon is a neutered male chicken weighing 5–8 pounds (2.5–4 kg). Capons have sweet, juicy flesh and are particularly good for roasting. You may need to order one in advance from the butcher. Mango juice is available in well-stocked supermarkets.

MAKES 6 SERVINGS

CUBING MANGO

Here is a quick way to cube a mango. On a cutting board, hold the mango upright on one of its narrow edges, and picture a long, flattened pit running lengthwise through the fruit. Just grazing the pit, cut off as large a slice as possible from each flat side of the mango. Score the cut side of each slice in a criss-cross grid pattern just down to the skin, then use your thumbs to push against the skin side, turning the slice inside out. Cut across the bottom of the cubes, releasing them from the skin. Trim any remaining flesh from the pit.

CHICKEN WITH CHILE AND LIME

HANDLING CHILES

The natural oils present in chiles can burn your fingers (and your eyes, if you rub them), so it's best to wear rubber or plastic gloves when handling the hotter ones. Trim away the stem end, cut the chile in half lengthwise, and strip out the seeds and ribs. Then slice, dice, or mince as directed. If you choose not to wear gloves, remember not to touch your face until after you have washed your hands thoroughly with soap and hot water.

Rinse the chicken under cold running water, discarding the giblets, and pat dry with paper towels. Remove and discard any loose fat.

To make the spice rub, combine the paprika, chili powder, thyme, garlic, and chile in a small bowl. Stir to blend.

Preheat the oven to 400°F (200°C). Place the chicken, breast side up, in an oiled heavy roasting pan just large enough to hold it comfortably. Rub the spice rub all over the outside of the chicken. Roast until the leg joints move easily and the juices run clear when a thigh is pierced with a knife, 50–60 minutes. An instant-read thermometer inserted into the thickest part of a thigh (but not touching bone) should read 170°F (77°C).

Transfer the chicken to a carving board, cover loosely with aluminum foil, and let stand for 10 minutes. Meanwhile, place the roasting pan, with the drippings, over medium-high heat and skim off the surface fat. Add the chicken stock and deglaze the pan, stirring with a wooden spoon to scrape up the browned bits from the bottom of the pan. Bring the liquid to a boil and cook until reduced by half, about 4 minutes. Season to taste with salt and pepper.

Carve the chicken (page 109) and arrange on a warmed platter. Sprinkle with the cilantro. Drizzle the pan sauce over the chicken and garnish with the lime slices. Serve at once.

Serving Tip: Serve with black beans and white rice.

MAKES 4 SERVINGS

1 fryer chicken, 3–3½ lb (1.5–1.75 kg)

FOR THE SPICE RUB:

2 tablespoons sweet Hungarian paprika

1 teaspoon chili powder

½ teaspoon dried thyme

2 cloves garlic, crushed

1 serrano chile, seeded and minced *(far left)*

¾ cup (6 fl oz/180 ml) chicken stock (page 110) or canned low-sodium broth

Salt and freshly ground pepper

½ cup (¾ oz/20 g) chopped fresh cilantro (fresh coriander)

2 limes, sliced

CORNISH HENS PROVENÇAL

4 Cornish hens, about 1 lb (500 g) each

3 tablespoons olive oil, plus extra for coating

Salt and freshly ground pepper

4 yellow summer squashes or zucchini (courgettes), sliced on the diagonal

1 large yellow onion, cut into wedges

2 cloves garlic, minced

3 tablespoons balsamic vinegar

2 teaspoons herbes de Provence

Mediterranean-style black olives for garnish (optional)

Preheat the oven to 425°F (220°C). Rinse the hens under cold running water, discarding the giblets, and pat dry with paper towels. Coat with olive oil and sprinkle inside and out with salt and pepper.

In a bowl, toss together the squashes, onion, garlic, the 3 tablespoons olive oil, vinegar, and herbes de Provence.

Place the hens, breast side up, in a roasting pan just large enough to hold them comfortably. Surround the hens with the vegetable mixture. Roast until the leg joints move easily and the juices run clear when a thigh is pierced with a knife, 35–45 minutes. An instant-read thermometer inserted into the thickest part of a thigh (but not touching bone) should read 170°F (77°C).

Transfer the hens to a carving board, cover loosely with aluminum foil, and let stand for 5 minutes. Arrange on warmed individual plates with the vegetables and garnish with black olives, if desired. Serve immediately.

MAKES 4 SERVINGS

HERBES DE PROVENCE

Available in specialty-food shops and well-stocked supermarkets, herbes de Provence is a dried herb blend that evokes the full-bodied flavors of southern French cooking. It typically includes thyme, summer savory, basil, fennel seeds, and lavender, and some versions may include a mix of sweet herbs such as marjoram with more pungent herbs such as rosemary and sage.

TURKEY BREAST WITH ROASTED PEARS

Preheat the oven to 400°F (200°C). Rinse the turkey breast under cold running water and pat dry with paper towels. Place the turkey breast, skin side up, in an oiled heavy roasting pan just large enough to hold it comfortably. Coat the breast with the melted butter and sprinkle to taste with salt and pepper.

Roast the turkey breast for 10 minutes. Reduce the oven temperature to 325°F (165°C) and continue roasting until the juices run clear when the thickest part of the turkey breast is pierced with a knife, about 1 hour and 25 or 35 minutes longer (for a total roasting time of 1 hour and 35 or 45 minutes). An instant-read thermometer inserted into the breast (but not touching bone) should read 165°F (74°C).

About 1 hour before the turkey is done, cut the pears in half lengthwise, core, and cut each half lengthwise in half again. In a large bowl, gently toss the pears with the orange juice and honey. Arrange the pears on top of and around the turkey breast. Turn them twice while roasting.

Transfer the turkey breast to a carving board, cover loosely with aluminum foil, and let stand for 10 minutes. Remove the pears and set aside. Thinly slice the turkey across the grain and arrange on a warmed platter. Skim the surface fat from the pan juices and spoon the juices over the turkey. Top and surround with the roasted pears and sprinkle with the pecans. Serve at once.

MAKES 8–10 SERVINGS

HONEY STYLES

The flavor of honey varies greatly, depending on what nectar the honeybees have gathered. Clover honey is one of the most common types, but depending on where you live, you might also be able to find acacia, eucalyptus, buckwheat, heather, sage, or other varieties. Wildflower honey (made from the nectar of various flowers) generally has a stronger flavor. Orange blossom honey is also delicious in this dish.

1 bone-in turkey breast, 5–6 lb (2.5–3 kg)

1–2 tablespoons unsalted butter, melted

Salt and freshly ground pepper

8 large firm, ripe pears such as Bosc or Anjou

¼ cup (2 fl oz/60 ml) fresh orange juice

¼ cup (3 oz/90 g) wild-flower honey or other fragrant honey

¼ cup (1 oz/30 g) chopped toasted pecans

CHINESE-STYLE DUCK

1 Long Island, or White Pekin, duck, 5–6 lb (2.5–3 kg)

¼ cup (3 oz/90 g) honey

1 teaspoon Chinese five-spice powder (page 113)

2 green (spring) onions, including tender green tops, cut into 2-inch (5-cm) pieces, plus sliced green tops for garnish

FOR THE DIPPING SAUCE:

¾ cup (6 fl oz/180 ml) hoisin sauce

1 tablespoon sugar

1 teaspoon Asian sesame oil

Rinse the duck under cold running water, discarding the giblets. Tie a piece of kitchen string around the duck under the wings, making a loop to be used to suspend the duck.

In a wok or large pot, bring 8 cups (2 l) water to a boil. Stir in the honey, five-spice powder, and green onions. Reduce the heat to a low simmer. Very carefully ease the duck into the water and poach for 6 minutes, turning once. Remove the duck and hang in a cool, airy, dry place, putting a large bowl or pan under it to catch any drips, until the duck is dry, 4–6 hours. (This poaching in hot liquid and air-drying helps to create a crisp skin during roasting.)

Meanwhile, make the dipping sauce. In a small saucepan, combine the hoisin sauce, sugar, and sesame oil. Cook over medium heat, stirring constantly, just until the ingredients are combined, about 1 minute. Spoon the sauce into a small bowl, cover, and refrigerate. Bring to room temperature before serving.

To roast the duck, place an oven rack in the lower third of the oven and preheat to 425°F (220°C).

Remove the string from the duck and discard. Pat the duck dry with paper towels. Place the duck, breast side up, on a rack in a roasting pan just large enough to hold it comfortably. Pour water into the pan to a depth of ½ inch (12 mm). Roast for 30 minutes. Reduce the oven temperature to 375°F (190°C). Continue roasting until the skin is crisp and the leg joints move easily, about 1 hour. An instant-read thermometer inserted into the thickest part of a thigh (but not touching bone) should read 180°F (82°C).

Transfer the duck to a carving board and let it rest for 10 minutes. Carve off the wings and drumsticks, then slice the remaining meat from the duck. Serve on a warmed platter, garnished with sliced green onion tops. Pass the dipping sauce at the table.

MAKES 4 SERVINGS

BLACK RICE

Rice is a classic accompaniment to this dish. For an interesting change, serve it with one of the exotic black rices on the market. Among them are black Japonica and Thai black sticky rices and black jasmine. All of them have a nutty flavor and a gorgeous hue ranging from light purple to almost black when cooked. You'll find various black rices or black rice blends in Chinese and Southeast Asian markets, natural-food stores, and well-stocked supermarkets.

GOOSE WITH ROASTED APPLES

Preheat the oven to 450°F (230°C). Rinse the goose under cold running water, discarding the giblets, and pat the bird dry with paper towels. Remove and discard any loose fat. Cut off the wing tips and the tail. Season the goose inside and out with salt and pepper. Prick the goose all over with a fork, piercing the skin but not the flesh. Loosely stuff the body cavity with the onion, celery, carrot, and apple.

Place the goose, breast side up, on a rack in a heavy roasting pan just large enough to hold it comfortably. Pour water into the roasting pan to a depth of ½ inch (12 mm). Roast the goose for 10 minutes. Reduce the oven temperature to 350°F (180°C). Continue roasting until the leg joints move easily and the juices run clear when a thigh is pierced with the tip of a knife, about 2½ hours longer (for a total roasting time of 2 hours and 40 minutes, or 20 minutes per pound). An instant-read thermometer inserted into the breast (but not touching bone) should read 175°–180°F (80°–82°C). Once during roasting, use a bulb baster to siphon out the accumulated drippings and then replace with water.

Meanwhile, prepare the apples. Halve the apples, core them, and cut the halves into quarters. Place the slices in a bowl, drizzle with the apple juice and vinegar, and sprinkle with the cinnamon and sugar. Toss the apples to coat evenly. About 20 minutes before the goose is ready, add the apples to the pan along with their liquid. Stir the apples once or twice during the remaining 20 minutes.

Transfer the goose to a carving board, cover loosely with aluminum foil, and let rest for 10 minutes. Remove the vegetables and apple from the cavity and discard them. Serve on a warmed platter with the roasted apple slices.

Serving Tip: For instructions on carving, see page 109.

Serving Tip: For instructions on carving, see page 109.

MAKES 6–8 SERVINGS

GOOSE FAT

Goose, like duck, has a thick layer of fat under the skin. To make the meat palatable, prick the skin all over before cooking to allow the fat to render off during roasting. You may want to save the rendered goose fat—it is a prized ingredient in French cooking, and potatoes or anything else fried in it taste delicious. Instead of discarding the pan juices, pour them into a jar and refrigerate. Scoop off the congealed fat and refrigerate it for up to 1 month. (Discard the remaining liquid.)

1 goose, about 8 lb (4 kg)

Salt and freshly ground pepper

1 yellow onion, thickly sliced

1 celery stalk, coarsely chopped

1 carrot, coarsely chopped

1 small unpeeled apple, cored and quartered

FOR THE ROASTED APPLES:

8–10 unpeeled small baking apples

1 cup (8 fl oz/250 ml) apple juice

2 tablespoons cider vinegar

½ teaspoon ground cinnamon

¾ cup (6 oz/185 g) sugar

BEEF, VEAL, AND VENISON

When it comes to meat, various roasting techniques apply. Lean cuts benefit from the tenderizing effect of a marinade or from being wrapped in bacon. Tender cuts, with their interior marbling of fat, stay juicy in the oven and may simply be roasted as they are. Finally, ground (minced) meat is mixed with bread crumbs and vegetables to produce a hearty meal worthy of second helpings.

FILETS MIGNONS WITH SHALLOTS AND POTATO WEDGES

Preheat the oven to 450°F (230°C). To make the potato wedges, cut each potato in half lengthwise, then cut each half lengthwise into 3 or 4 wedges. In a large, shallow roasting pan, toss the potato wedges with the olive oil to coat. Spread in a single layer and sprinkle with the thyme. Roast, turning once or twice, until fork-tender, 40–50 minutes. Remove from the oven and cover loosely with aluminum foil to keep warm.

Meanwhile, pat the filets dry with paper towels. Select a shallow roasting pan or baking sheet just large enough to hold the filets comfortably. Line it with aluminum foil and oil the foil. Add the shallots to the pan and toss with the melted butter to coat.

Coat the filets with oil and season with salt and pepper. Place a dry large frying pan, preferably cast iron, over high heat. When very hot, lightly sprinkle the pan with salt (see Note). Brown the filets in batches, turning once, just until nicely colored, 5–6 minutes per batch. Transfer the filets to the roasting pan and arrange at least 2 inches (5 cm) apart on top of the shallots.

When the potatoes are out of the oven, raise the oven temperature to 475°F (245°C). Roast the filets until an instant-read thermometer inserted into the center of a filet reads 125°F (52°C) for rare, about 7 minutes total.

Transfer the filets to a cutting board, loosely cover with aluminum foil, and let stand for 5 minutes. Arrange on warmed individual plates with the shallots and potato wedges and serve.

Note: Sprinkling salt in the hot frying pan before searing the filets will help prevent the filets from sticking to the pan.

MAKES 6 SERVINGS

FOR THE POTATO WEDGES:

4 unpeeled russet potatoes, scrubbed

2 tablespoons extra-virgin olive oil

Minced fresh thyme or dried thyme for sprinkling

6 filets mignons, each about 6 oz (185 g) and 1¼ inches (3 cm) thick

2 cups (10 oz/315 g) sliced shallots (about 20 large shallots)

2 tablespoons unsalted butter, melted

Extra-virgin olive oil for coating

Salt and freshly ground pepper

STANDING RIB ROAST WITH YORKSHIRE PUDDING

1 standing rib roast,
6–6½ lb (3–3.25 kg)

FOR THE YORKSHIRE
PUDDING:

3 eggs

1 cup (8 fl oz/250 ml) milk

1 cup (5 oz/155 g)
all-purpose (plain) flour

½ teaspoon salt

2 tablespoons fat from
roasting pan

¾ cup (6 fl oz/180 ml)
dry red wine

Salt and freshly ground
pepper

Place a rack in the lower third of the oven and preheat to 450°F (230°C). Place the roast, fat side up, in an oiled flameproof heavy roasting pan just large enough to hold it comfortably. Roast for 20 minutes, then reduce the oven temperature to 350°F (180°C). Continue roasting until an instant-read thermometer inserted into the center of the roast reads 125°–130°F (52°–54°C) for rare to medium-rare, about 1 hour and 10 minutes longer (for a total roasting time of 1½ hours).

While the meat is roasting, make the batter for the Yorkshire pudding. In a bowl, whisk together the eggs and milk. Whisk in the flour and salt. Pour into a small pitcher, cover, and refrigerate.

Transfer the cooked roast to a carving board and cover loosely with aluminum foil. Let rest while baking the pudding.

To make the pudding, raise the oven temperature to 450°F (230°C). Skim the surface fat from the drippings, reserving both the fat and the pan with the drippings. Spoon 2 tablespoons of the fat into a metal pie pan or baking pan and put the pan in the oven until it is very hot, about 4 minutes. Pour the batter into the hot pan. Bake on the lower rack until the pudding is golden and puffed, about 20 minutes, rotating once if puffing unevenly.

Meanwhile, place the roasting pan with the drippings over medium heat. Pour in the wine and deglaze the pan, stirring to scrape up the browned bits. Continue cooking until the liquid is reduced by half, about 5 minutes. Season to taste with salt and pepper. Pour into a sauce boat.

Just before the pudding is ready, slice the beef and arrange on a warmed platter. Serve with the pudding and sauce.

MAKES 6–8 SERVINGS

YORKSHIRE PUDDING

This savory "pudding" is made from the same batter as popovers, but instead of being poured into individual cups, it is made as one large soufflélike bread. The key to a good Yorkshire pudding is to have both the pan and the fat very hot when you pour in the batter. This immediately cooks the batter as it comes into contact with the pan and puffs up the pudding nicely. Serve Yorkshire pudding directly from the oven, as it will quickly deflate.

SHORT RIBS WITH LEEKS AND SPINACH

Preheat the oven to 350°F (180°C). In a dry large frying pan over medium heat, brown the ribs in batches, turning often, until nicely colored, 8–10 minutes per batch. Transfer the ribs to an oiled heavy roasting pan just large enough to hold all of them comfortably.

In a bowl, combine the leeks, garlic, stock, ketchup, and salt and pepper to taste. Stir to blend and pour over the ribs.

Roast the ribs for 30 minutes. Stir in the spinach, mixing it well. Continue roasting until the ribs are fork-tender, 15–30 minutes longer.

Transfer the ribs to a warmed large shallow bowl with the pan juices and vegetables and serve hot.

Serving Tip: Serve a green salad alongside this hearty dish.

MAKES 6 SERVINGS

6 lb (3 kg) beef short ribs

2 large leeks, white parts only, sliced crosswise

4 cloves garlic

1 cup (8 fl oz/250 ml) beef stock (page 110) or canned low-sodium broth

½ cup (4½ oz/140 g) ketchup

Salt and freshly ground pepper

1 bunch spinach, cleaned and stemmed

CLEANING LEEKS

These long, bulbous green and white members of the onion branch of the *Allium* genus are grown in sandy soil and often have dirt trapped among their many layers. Leeks should be carefully rinsed, either before or after slicing. For this recipe, use a sharp knife to cut off the green tops and stringy roots. Cut the white part of the leek into slices ¼ inch (6 mm) thick, then immerse the pieces in a bowl of cold water to dislodge any sand. Spinach, also grown in sand, should similarly be immersed and carefully cleaned.

EYE OF ROUND SANDWICHES

1 eye of round beef roast, about 4½ lb (2.25 kg)

6 oz (185 g) sliced bacon

1 bunch fresh dill, stemmed

Sandwich rolls such as onion rolls, croissants, or potato bread rolls, split horizontally

Stone-ground mustard

Tomato slices

Lettuce leaves

Red onion slices

Dill pickles

Preheat the oven to 450°F (230°C). Wrap the roast with the bacon slices and set the roast in an oiled roasting pan just large enough to hold it comfortably. Arrange a few sprigs of dill over the meat.

Roast for 15 minutes. Reduce the oven temperature to 400°F (200°C) and continue roasting until an instant-read thermometer inserted into the thickest part of the roast reads 125°F (52°C) for rare, about 1 hour longer (for a total roasting time of 1¼ hours).

Transfer the roast to a carving board, cover loosely with aluminum foil, and let stand for 10 minutes. Remove and crumble the bacon. Slice the meat thinly against the grain, arrange on a warmed platter, and sprinkle with the bacon bits. Surround with the remaining dill. Serve with a basket of rolls and with mustard, tomatoes, lettuce leaves, red onions, and pickles, allowing diners to make their own sandwiches.

MAKES 10–12 SERVINGS

DILL

This delicate herb is treasured for more than its appealingly bright, somewhat grassy flavor. Dill is a natural preservative, which is why it's used in making pickles and curing salmon. It's also considered a digestive herb, and cooled dill tea was once a popular folk remedy for infant colic. Fresh dill is available in many markets.

MEAT LOAF WITH ONIONS AND CARROTS

Preheat the oven to 350°F (180°C). In a saucepan, over medium-high heat, warm the olive oil. Add the chopped onion, bell pepper, and garlic and sauté, stirring occasionally, until softened, about 5 minutes. Transfer the onion mixture to a large bowl and stir in the hot-pepper sauce, Worcestershire sauce, mustard, water, and bread crumbs. Add the ground beef, eggs, ½ teaspoon salt, and ¼ teaspoon pepper. Stir to blend well.

Spoon the mixture into a 9-by-5-inch (23-by-13-cm) loaf pan, packing it into a compact loaf. Bake until cooked through, about 1 hour.

Meanwhile, in a frying pan over medium heat, melt the butter. Add the sliced onions and shredded carrots and cook, stirring occasionally, until tender, about 5 minutes. Season to taste with salt and pepper.

Remove the meat loaf from the oven and let stand for 5 minutes. Slice and serve with the onions and carrots.

Serving Tip: Serve with mashed potatoes.

Variation Tip: Hard-boil 2 eggs (page 113), let cool, and then peel. Spoon half of the meat mixture into the loaf pan, lay the eggs, end to end, down the center, and spoon in the remaining meat mixture. Compact the mixture tightly, then bake as directed.

MAKES 8 SERVINGS

PREPARING GARLIC

To mince a clove of garlic, trim off both ends of the clove, then loosen the papery skin by crushing the clove lightly with the flat side of a large knife, using the heel of your palm to apply the pressure. Remove the skin and chop the garlic into fine pieces. If a garlic clove has a green sprout formed in its center, the garlic is a little past its prime. You can still use it, but halve the clove lengthwise before mincing and remove the sprout, which tastes bitter. Garlic will also taste bitter if it is burned, so watch carefully while it cooks.

2 tablespoons olive oil

3 yellow onions, 1 chopped and 2 sliced

1 green bell pepper (capsicum), seeded and chopped

2 cloves garlic, minced

¼ cup (2 fl oz/60 ml) hot-pepper sauce

2 teaspoons Worcestershire sauce

2 tablespoons stone-ground mustard

½ cup (4 fl oz/125 ml) water

½ cup (2 oz/60 g) dried whole-wheat (wholemeal) bread crumbs (page 70)

2 lb (1 kg) ground (minced) beef chuck

2 eggs, lightly beaten

Salt and freshly ground pepper

3 tablespoons unsalted butter

2 carrots, peeled and shredded

HERB-ENCRUSTED BREAST OF VEAL

1 bone-in veal breast,
5½–6 lb (2.75–3 kg),
pocket cut in top section
(far right)

FOR THE STUFFING:

2 tablespoons unsalted
butter

1 yellow onion, chopped

3 cloves garlic, minced

¾ cup (1 oz/30 g) minced
fresh flat-leaf (Italian)
parsley

2 cups (8 oz/250 g) dried
bread crumbs (page 70)

1¼ lb (625 g) ground
(minced) veal

2 eggs, lightly beaten

Salt and ground pepper

Olive oil for coating

Salt and freshly ground
pepper

2 teaspoons dried thyme

1 teaspoon dried basil

½ teaspoon sweet
Hungarian paprika

1 large yellow onion

4 large carrots, peeled

6 unpeeled russet
potatoes, well scrubbed

Preheat the oven to 350°F (180°C). If not already done by the butcher, cut a pocket in the top section of the veal breast.

To make the stuffing, melt the butter over medium heat in a frying pan. Add the onion and garlic and sauté until translucent, about 5 minutes. Remove from the heat and transfer to a bowl. Mix in the parsley, bread crumbs, ground veal, eggs, and salt and pepper to taste. Stir to blend.

Coat the veal breast with oil and season inside and out with salt and pepper. Stuff the bread crumb mixture into the veal pocket. Truss the veal to keep the stuffing from falling out, tying the meat closed with kitchen string. Place the veal, bone side down, in an oiled heavy roasting pan just large enough to hold it comfortably. Sprinkle the veal with the thyme, basil, and paprika.

Cut the onion into wedges, cut the carrots on the diagonal into slices ½ inch (12 mm) thick, and cut each potato into 6 wedges about ¾ inch (2 cm) thick. Arrange the vegetables around the veal.

Roast, basting occasionally, until fork-tender, about 2 hours, depending on the weight of the veal. An instant-read thermometer inserted into the center of the veal should read 160°F (71°C). Do not overcook; the meat should be moist. Turn the vegetables 2 or 3 times during roasting.

Transfer the veal to a carving board, cover loosely with aluminum foil, and let rest for 10 minutes. Slice the veal between the ribs, cutting through the cartilage that joins the bones. Arrange on warmed individual plates with the vegetables. Serve hot.

Note: Breast of veal is not a cut you see every day, but it makes a delicious roast. Check with the butcher to see whether this cut needs to be ordered in advance.

MAKES 6 SERVINGS

STUFFING VEAL BREAST

Breast of veal, with its interior fat marbling, is a good cut for roasting and is traditionally stuffed. To prepare the breast for stuffing, cut a horizontal pocket in the top section of the breast parallel to the bones. Trussing the veal breast will help to keep its shape and makes it easier to carve. For more information on trussing, see page 106.

TENDERLOIN OF VENISON WITH BLUEBERRIES

To make the marinade, combine the wine, olive oil, orange juice, green onion, bay leaves, and pepper in a bowl. Mix well.

Place the venison tenderloins in a large zippered plastic bag and add the marinade. Seal the bag and place it on a plate or in a bowl. Refrigerate for 24–36 hours, turning the bag occasionally to coat the venison with the marinade. Remove the venison from the refrigerator 30 minutes before roasting and drain well, discarding the marinade.

Preheat the oven to 375°F (190°C). Place the venison tenderloins in an oiled roasting pan just large enough to hold them comfortably. Brush the tenderloins with the melted butter and sprinkle with salt and pepper. Scatter 1 cup (4 oz/125 g) of the blueberries over the meat (they will mostly fall to the side).

Roast the venison until an instant-read thermometer inserted into the meat reads 125°F (52°C) for rare, about 40 minutes.

Transfer the tenderloins to a carving board, cover loosely with aluminum foil, and let rest for 10 minutes.

Meanwhile, make the sauce. Combine the blueberries from the roasting pan, Port, and blueberry jam in a small saucepan. Place over medium heat and cook, stirring occasionally, just until the jam melts.

Slice the venison thinly against the grain and arrange on a warmed platter. Drizzle the sauce over the venison, sprinkle with the remaining 2 cups (8 oz/250 g) uncooked blueberries, and serve.

Note: Venison is best when not cooked past medium-rare. When well done, it toughens and develops a gamy flavor.

Serving Tip: This dish is good with roasted parsnips (page 99).

MAKES 4 SERVINGS

MARINATING

A marinade serves to flavor food and to tenderize it. Herbs, spices, garlic, and other flavorful ingredients are almost always included, and an acid such as wine or citrus juice acts as a tenderizer. A tougher meat such as venison benefits from long marinating. The easiest way to do it is to combine the meat and marinade in a zippered plastic bag, turn the sealed bag in all directions to coat the food well, and then place it in a shallow bowl and refrigerate. Turn the bag occasionally to coat the food evenly with the marinade. Remove from the refrigerator at least 30 minutes before roasting.

FOR THE MARINADE:

2 cups (16 fl oz/500 ml) dry red wine

¾ cup (6 fl oz/180 ml) olive oil

½ cup (4 fl oz/125 ml) fresh orange juice

1 green (spring) onion, including tender green tops, finely chopped

3 bay leaves

½ teaspoon freshly ground pepper

2 venison tenderloins, about 1½ lb (750 g) total weight

2 tablespoons unsalted butter, melted

Salt and freshly ground pepper

3 cups (12 oz/375 g) fresh or thawed frozen blueberries

FOR THE SAUCE:

½ cup (4 fl oz/125 ml) Port

⅓ cup (3 oz/90 g) blueberry jam

PORK AND LAMB

Rich in flavor, pork and lamb rank high among the best meats for roasting. Baby back ribs cooked slowly in the oven and smothered with barbecue sauce can be a special treat any time of year, and a pork tenderloin is not only delicious, but also surprisingly lean. The delicious, distinct flavor of roasted lamb pairs beautifully with mint and other herbs.

PORK TENDERLOIN
WITH GLAZED SWEET ONIONS
58

COUSCOUS-STUFFED PORK CHOPS
61

BABY BACK RIBS
WITH BARBECUE SAUCE
62

SPICE-RUBBED PORK LOIN
WITH RATATOUILLE
65

HAM WITH ORANGE GLAZE
66

RACK OF LAMB WITH MINT SAUCE
69

SADDLE OF LAMB
WITH FLAVORED BREAD CRUMBS
70

PORK TENDERLOIN
WITH GLAZED SWEET ONIONS

Preheat the oven to 375°F (190°C). In a large frying pan over medium heat, melt the butter. Add the onions and sauté until softened, about 2 minutes. Stir in the brown sugar, vinegar, raisins, and salt and pepper to taste and cook until the onions are tender and glazed, about 3 minutes.

Arrange the pork tenderloins in an oiled roasting pan just large enough to hold them comfortably. Spoon the glazed onions over the pork. Roast the pork until browned on the outside and just faintly pink in the center, about 45 minutes. An instant-read thermometer inserted into the pork should read 155°–160°F (68°–71°C).

Transfer the pork tenderloins to a carving board, cover loosely with aluminum foil, and let stand for 5 minutes. Slice and serve on warmed individual plates with the glazed onions.

MAKES 8 SERVINGS

2 tablespoons unsalted butter

2 large Vidalia or other sweet onions, sliced

2 tablespoons firmly packed dark brown sugar

2 tablespoons balsamic vinegar

½ cup (3 oz/90 g) golden raisins (sultanas) or chopped dried apricots

Salt and freshly ground pepper

2 pork tenderloins, about 1 lb (500 g) each

SWEET ONIONS

Some varieties of onion are especially mild and gain sweetness as they cook. Grown in southeast Georgia, the Vidalia is the best-known sweet onion of the American South. It shares an ancestry with other sweet onions, such as the Maui from Hawaii, the Walla Walla from Washington, and the Granos from Texas. Any sweet onion may be used in this recipe.

COUSCOUS-STUFFED PORK CHOPS

FOR THE STUFFING:

1¼ cups (10 fl oz/310 ml) plus 3 tablespoons chicken stock (page 110) or canned low-sodium broth

5 tablespoons (2½ oz/ 75 g) unsalted butter

¾ cup (4 oz/125 g) couscous

1 small yellow onion, finely chopped

2 cloves garlic, minced

½ cup (3 oz/90 g) dried currants

½ cup (2½ oz/75 g) pine nuts

⅛ teaspoon ground cinnamon

Salt and freshly ground pepper

6 boneless pork loin chops, about 2½ lb (1.25 kg) total weight, butterflied *(far right)*

Orange marmalade for coating

To make the stuffing, combine the 1¼ cups chicken stock and 2 tablespoons of the butter in a saucepan. Bring to a boil over medium heat. Stir in the couscous. Remove from the heat, cover, and let stand for 5 minutes. Uncover the couscous and fluff it with a fork.

In a frying pan over medium heat, melt the remaining 3 tablespoons butter. Add the onion and garlic and sauté until tender, about 5 minutes. Remove from the heat and stir in the currants, pine nuts, couscous, cinnamon, ½ teaspoon salt, and ¼ teaspoon pepper. Toss the mixture with as much of the remaining 3 tablespoons chicken stock as needed to hold it together slightly.

Preheat the oven to 350°F (180°C). Stuff each chop generously with stuffing and insert toothpicks to keep the chops closed. Reserve about ⅓ cup (2 oz/60 g) stuffing to sprinkle over the chops. Place the pork chops in an oiled roasting pan just large enough to hold them comfortably and coat them generously with the marmalade. Sprinkle with the reserved stuffing and press it lightly into the marmalade so that it will stick to the chops.

Roast until the chops are browned on the outside, but just slightly pink in the center, 40–45 minutes.

Transfer the pork chops to warmed individual plates, remove the toothpicks, and serve hot.

Serving Tip: Serve with buttered warm pita bread and roasted bell peppers (capsicums) (page 22).

MAKES 6 SERVINGS

BUTTERFLYING

Butterflied pork chops are sold in most supermarkets and meat markets, but if they're not available, you can easily butterfly them yourself. Buy boneless loin chops that are at least 1 inch (2.5 cm) thick. Holding a knife parallel to the cutting board and starting at the rounded side, slice the meat horizontally almost all the way through to the other side, stopping about 1 inch (2.5 cm) short. Open the meat up flat, like a book—or a butterfly.

BABY BACK RIBS
WITH BARBECUE SAUCE

BARBECUE SAUCE STYLES
In eastern North Carolina, it's a vinegary red pepper sauce. In South Carolina, it's seasoned with mustard. In Kansas City, it's a sweet tomato sauce. American barbecue sauces vary from place to place, but tomato-based sauces are popular throughout most of the country. The sauce usually contains acid (from vinegar or tomatoes) for a bit of tenderness, spices for flavor, and sugar, which caramelizes at high heat, lending a smoky sweetness to meats and poultry.

To make the barbecue sauce, in a saucepan over medium heat, heat the peanut oil. Add the onion, garlic, and chile and sauté until the onion is translucent, about 5 minutes. Add the tomatoes and their juice, the Worcestershire sauce, brown sugar, vinegar, cumin, and salt. Bring to a boil over medium heat, reduce the heat to low, and simmer, stirring occasionally, for 5 minutes to blend the flavors. Taste and adjust the seasoning. Remove from the heat and let cool.

Preheat the oven to 350°F (180°C). Cut the ribs into serving-sized pieces of 6–8 rib sections each. Arrange the ribs on a rack in a roasting pan large enough to hold them comfortably (stack them if needed) and pour 2 cups (16 fl oz/500 ml) water into the pan. Cover the pan tightly with heavy-duty aluminum foil. Bake the ribs for 45 minutes. Remove the pan from the oven, uncover, and brush the ribs on both sides with the sauce. Roast, uncovered, until fork-tender, about 15 minutes longer (for a total roasting time of 1 hour). Remove from the oven. Brush the ribs generously with sauce on both sides. Let stand for 5 minutes.

Serve hot, passing the remaining barbecue sauce at the table.

Serving Tip: Serve these ribs with corn bread and coleslaw.

Make-Ahead Tip: The barbecue sauce may be made 1–2 days before serving. Transfer the sauce to a nonaluminum bowl, cover, and refrigerate. Reheat over medium heat to take the chill off. If you're in a hurry, use a good bottled sauce and spice it up with sautéed garlic and chiles, hot-pepper sauce, or whatever else you like.

MAKES 6 SERVINGS

FOR THE BARBECUE SAUCE:

3 tablespoons peanut oil

1 yellow onion, chopped

4 cloves garlic, minced

1 jalapeño chile, seeded and sliced (page 30)

1½ cups (9 oz/280 g) canned diced tomatoes, including juice

1 teaspoon Worcestershire sauce

¼ cup (2 oz/60 g) firmly packed light brown sugar

¼ cup (2 fl oz/60 ml) red wine vinegar

1 teaspoon ground cumin

¼ teaspoon salt

6 lb (3 kg) baby back ribs, in slabs

SPICE-RUBBED PORK LOIN
WITH RATATOUILLE

FOR THE SPICE RUB:

½ teaspoon dried oregano

½ teaspoon garlic powder

⅛ teaspoon freshly ground
pepper

1 boneless pork loin roast,
about 3 lb (1.5 kg)

3 tomatoes, coarsely
chopped

3 baby globe eggplants
(aubergines), peeled and
cut into chunks

1 zucchini (courgette), cut
into chunks

1 red or green bell pepper
(capsicum), seeded and
cut into chunks

1 yellow onion,
cut into chunks

3 cloves garlic, minced

2 teaspoons minced fresh
basil or 1 teaspoon dried

Salt and freshly ground
pepper

2 tablespoons capers,
including brine

Preheat the oven to 400°F (200°C). To make the spice rub, combine the oregano, garlic powder, and pepper in a small bowl.

Pat the pork dry with paper towels and rub all over with the spice rub. Place the pork in an oiled heavy roasting pan just large enough to hold it comfortably.

Arrange the tomatoes, eggplants, zucchini, bell pepper, and onion around the pork. Sprinkle with the garlic, basil, and salt and pepper to taste. Scatter the capers over all.

Roast the pork until it is cooked through but still slightly pink in the center, about 1½ hours. An instant-read thermometer inserted into the pork should read 155°–160°F (68°–71°C). Turn the vegetables twice during roasting.

Transfer the pork to a carving board, cover loosely with aluminum foil, and let stand for 10 minutes. Slice and arrange on a warmed platter. Surround with the vegetables and serve.

MAKES 6 SERVINGS

EGGPLANT

Eggplants (aubergines) come in a range of shapes and sizes, from barely bigger than an egg—and the same ivory color—to the familiar large purple globe variety. Baby eggplants look like their larger kin but are smaller, generally 3–5 inches (7.5–13 cm) long. They are thinner-skinned than large eggplants and less likely to be bitter. Other alternatives for this dish are slender dark purple Asian eggplants or the slender pale lavender variety known as Chinese eggplants.

HAM WITH ORANGE GLAZE

Preheat the oven to 350°F (180°C). Using a small knife, remove the skin from the ham, leaving a layer of fat about ¼ inch (6 mm) thick. Set the ham, fat side up, in an oiled heavy roasting pan just large enough to hold it comfortably. Roast the ham for 1 hour.

Meanwhile, to make the glaze, combine the orange marmalade and orange juice in a small saucepan. Cook over low heat, stirring frequently, until the marmalade is melted. Remove from the heat and stir in the sherry and mustard.

Remove the ham from the oven and score the fat in a diamond pattern. Stud the center of each diamond with a clove, if desired. Brush the ham with the orange glaze. Return the ham to the oven and roast until completely heated through, about 1 hour longer. An instant-read thermometer inserted into the ham should read 160°F (71°C). Brush the ham with glaze twice during the last hour of cooking.

Remove the ham from the oven, transfer to a carving board, cover loosely with aluminum foil, and let rest for 10 minutes. Let the pan juices cool for 5 minutes, then pour into a small saucepan and skim off the fat. Cook over medium-low heat until heated through, 2–3 minutes.

Slice the ham and arrange on a warmed platter. Pour the warm pan juices into a bowl and serve alongside the ham.

Serving Tip: This ham is good served with sweet potatoes and biscuits with honey.

MAKES ABOUT 16 SERVINGS

HAM STYLES

The ham used in this recipe is wet-cured, which means that it has been soaked in or injected with brine during curing. Dry-cured hams such as American Smithfield, Italian prosciutto, or German Black Forest ham are a different style of ham and should not be roasted in the manner described in this recipe. When buying a wet-cured ham, choose those labeled as cured "with natural juices" rather than "with added water." Bone-in hams stay juicier and taste better than boneless hams, and the shank end of a ham is more flavorful than the butt end.

1 bone-in partially cooked wet-cured shank-end ham, 6–8 lb (3–4 kg)

FOR THE ORANGE GLAZE:

1 cup (10 oz/315 g) orange marmalade

2 tablespoons fresh orange juice

¼ cup (2 fl oz/60 ml) cream sherry

¼ cup (2 oz/60 g) mild mustard

Whole cloves for studding ham (optional)

RACK OF LAMB WITH MINT SAUCE

FOR THE SPICE RUB:

2 tablespoons firmly packed
dark brown sugar

½ teaspoon freshly ground
pepper

1 tablespoon ground
cardamom

½ teaspoon ground
cinnamon

2 racks of lamb, each with
7 or 8 ribs, 1½–1¾ lb
(750–875 g) total weight

FOR THE MINT SAUCE:

½ cup (½ oz/15 g) packed
fresh mint leaves

2 tablespoons confectioners'
(icing) sugar

⅓ cup (3 fl oz/90 ml)
cider vinegar or rice
wine vinegar

To make the spice rub, combine the brown sugar, pepper, cardamom, and cinnamon in a small bowl. Stir to blend.

Rub the racks of lamb all over with the spice rub. Put the lamb on a plate, cover, and let sit at room temperature for at least 30 minutes or for up to 2 hours.

Preheat the oven to 475°F (245°C). Place the racks of lamb in an oiled roasting pan just large enough to hold them comfortably. Roast for 10 minutes. Reduce the oven temperature to 375°F (190°C) and continue roasting the lamb until an instant-read thermometer inserted into the rack (but not touching bone) reads 125°F (52°C) for rare, 10–15 minutes. Transfer the lamb to a carving board, cover loosely with aluminum foil, and let stand for 5 minutes.

While the lamb is roasting, make the mint sauce. Combine the mint, confectioners' sugar, and vinegar in a blender or mini food processor and process until the mint is minced. Spoon into a small glass bowl. Set aside.

Cut the lamb into individual rib chops and arrange on warmed individual plates. Serve hot, drizzled with the mint sauce.

Serving Tip: Serve with roasted asparagus (page 88) and potato wedges (page 42).

MAKES 4 SERVINGS

MINT

This tender herb loses most of its vibrant flavor when dried; whenever possible, use it fresh. The herb labeled "mint" in the supermarket will be either peppermint or spearmint. Of the two, peppermint has the sharper flavor. To store fresh mint, trim off the bottoms of the stems and place the sprigs in a glass of water, just as you would fresh flowers. Cover the mint loosely with a plastic bag and store in the refrigerator for up to 1 week. (This storage method also works well for parsley and cilantro/fresh coriander.)

SADDLE OF LAMB
WITH FLAVORED BREAD CRUMBS

MAKING BREAD CRUMBS

Making fresh bread crumbs is an ideal use for leftover bread. For this recipe, trim the crusts from 2 slices of day-old French bread or other white bread, tear the bread into pieces, and place in a food processor. Pulse to process into fine crumbs. This makes about 1 cup (2 oz/ 60 g) fresh crumbs. For dried bread crumbs, let the bread slices dry out in a 200°F (95°C) oven for about 1 hour. Break the bread into pieces and place in a food processor. Pulse to process into fine crumbs. Sourdough and country-style loaves also make good crumbs.

Place an oven rack in the lower third of the oven and preheat the oven to 375°F (190°C). Put the lamb in an oiled flameproof heavy roasting pan just large enough to hold it comfortably, sprinkle generously with salt and pepper, and place it in the oven.

Shortly after the lamb goes in the oven, make the flavored bread crumbs. In a bowl, toss the crumbs with the parsley, shallots, and garlic. Stir in the melted butter. Remove the lamb from the oven after 40–45 minutes of roasting and spread the crumbs on top, gently pressing them in. Return the lamb to the oven and continue roasting, basting twice with the pan juices, until an instant-read thermometer inserted in the lamb reads 125°F (52°C) for rare, 45–50 minutes longer (for a total roasting time of 1½ hours). Transfer the lamb to a carving board, cover loosely with aluminum foil, and let rest for 10 minutes.

Meanwhile, place the roasting pan, with the drippings, over medium-high heat and skim off the surface fat. Add the wine and deglaze the pan, stirring to scrape up the browned bits from the bottom of the pan. Bring the liquid to a boil and cook until reduced by half, about 4 minutes. Season to taste with salt and pepper.

Slice the lamb and serve on warmed individual plates along with the sauce.

Note: Saddle of lamb is a good choice for special occasions or holiday dinners. Check with the butcher to see whether this roast needs to be ordered in advance.

MAKES 6 SERVINGS

1 saddle of lamb, 4½–6 lb (2.25–3 kg), boned, trimmed of fat, and tied

Salt and freshly ground pepper

FOR THE FLAVORED BREAD CRUMBS:

¾ cup (1½ oz/45 g) fresh white bread crumbs *(far left)*

¼ cup (⅓ oz/10 g) minced fresh flat-leaf (Italian) parsley

2 shallots, minced

1 clove garlic, minced

4 tablespoons (2 oz/60 g) unsalted butter, melted

½ cup (4 fl oz/125 ml) dry red wine

FISH AND SHELLFISH

Although roasting may not be the cooking method that first comes to mind when you think of fish and seafood, it is an excellent way to prepare them. When roasted quickly at high temperatures, everything from halibut and sea bass to shrimp and oysters yields tender and succulent results.

JUMBO SHRIMP
WITH SPICY AVOCADO SAUCE
74

OYSTER ROAST WITH CAVIAR
77

TROUT WITH HORSERADISH CRUMBS
78

SEA BASS WITH FENNEL AND PERNOD
81

HALIBUT STEAKS AU POIVRE
82

BLUEFISH WITH TOMATO BUTTER
85

JUMBO SHRIMP
WITH SPICY AVOCADO SAUCE

To make the avocado sauce, combine the avocados, tomato, onion, chile, lime juice, and salt in a food processor and pulse to form a chunky purée. Spoon the mixture into a bowl, cover, and set aside.

Preheat the oven to 400°F (200°C). Line a small baking pan with aluminum foil and oil the foil. Arrange the shrimp in the prepared pan, brush with the hot-pepper sauce, and sprinkle with cumin seeds.

Roast the shrimp, turning once, until they are evenly pink and firm to the touch, 3–3½ minutes on each side. Line small individual plates with the lettuce leaves and top with the shrimp. Place a dollop of the avocado sauce on each serving.

MAKES 6 FIRST-COURSE SERVINGS

PREPARING AVOCADOS

The avocado is a tropical fruit treasured for its rich, buttery flesh. To prepare an avocado, first cut it in half lengthwise with a small, sharp knife, cutting around the pit. Rotate the halves in opposite directions to separate them. Use a spoon to lift out the pit, or carefully strike the pit with the blade of a very sharp knife so that the blade lodges in it and pull out the pit. Use criss-cross strokes to cut the flesh into chunks, then use a large spoon to scoop the flesh from the skin.

FOR THE AVOCADO SAUCE:

2 ripe avocados, halved, pitted, and cut into chunks *(far left)*

1 tomato, peeled (page 18) and cut into chunks

1 small white onion, coarsely chopped

1 jalapeño chile, seeded and finely chopped (page 30)

2 tablespoons fresh lime juice

¼ teaspoon salt

18 jumbo shrimp (prawns), peeled and deveined

¼ cup (2 fl oz/60 ml) hot-pepper sauce

Cumin seeds for sprinkling

Lettuce leaves for serving

OYSTER ROAST WITH CAVIAR

Rock salt

24 large oysters, shucked and on the half shell *(far right)*

6 tablespoons (3 oz/90 g) unsalted butter, melted

Juice from 2 lemons

2 oz (60 g) caviar, salmon roe, and/or whitefish roe

Preheat the oven to 450°F (230°C). Pour enough rock salt into the bottom of a gratin dish just large enough to hold the oysters (or use 2 dishes) to create an even layer 1 inch (2.5 cm) thick.

Arrange the oysters in their half shells on top of the salt. Brush the oysters with the melted butter. Roast just until the oysters are hot and beginning to curl, 5–6 minutes. Remove from the oven, sprinkle with the lemon juice, and spoon a dollop of caviar on top of each oyster. Serve the oysters still on their bed of salt.

Note: Once shucked, oysters are highly perishable; plan to roast them immediately.

Serving Tip: Serve these roasted oysters with buttered thin slices of dark rye bread.

MAKES 6 FIRST-COURSE SERVINGS

SHUCKING OYSTERS

To shuck an oyster, grasp it, flat top shell facing up, with a kitchen towel or metal-mesh glove in your nondominant hand. Holding an oyster knife in your other hand, insert the knife tip between the shells about ½ inch (12 mm) from the hinge. Twist the knife to loosen the top shell. Run the knife carefully along the inside surface of the top shell, severing the muscle that grips it. Take care not to cut the oyster or to spill its liquor. Discard the top shell. Slide the knife under the oyster, loosening it from the bottom shell.

TROUT WITH HORSERADISH CRUMBS

To make the horseradish crumbs, put the bread crumbs in a bowl with the butter, horseradish, and chives and toss to combine.

Preheat the oven to 450°F (230°C). Rinse the trout under cold running water and pat dry with paper towels. Make 3 deep diagonal cuts on one side of each trout. Coat with most of the melted butter and sprinkle to taste with salt and pepper. Choose a roasting pan just large enough to hold the trout comfortably, or use 2 pans. Coat the bottom of the pan(s) with the remaining melted butter. Arrange the trout, slashed side up, in the pan(s). Sprinkle with the crumb mixture, spreading it evenly and gently pressing it into the cuts.

Roast the trout until the crumbs are lightly browned and the fish flakes easily when the flesh in the slashes is prodded gently with a fork, 15–20 minutes. Transfer to a platter, garnish with the chive lengths, and serve at once.

Serving Tip: Accompany with roasted asparagus (page 88).

MAKES 6 SERVINGS

HORSERADISH

Prepared horseradish with white vinegar is widely available in jars in the refrigerated section of the supermarket. If you can find fresh horseradish root, try preparing it to make this dish. Peel the root, cut it into slices, and purée it in a food processor. Add white vinegar to taste and process to make a paste. Remove the cover of the processor, turning it away from you to avoid the strong horseradish fumes. Spoon the horseradish into a covered container and refrigerate until ready to use.

FOR THE HORSERADISH CRUMBS:

2 cups (8 oz/250 g) dried white bread crumbs (page 70)

6 tablespoons (3 oz/90 g) unsalted butter, melted

2 tablespoons prepared horseradish *(far left)*

2 tablespoons minced fresh chives

6 small rainbow trout, ¾–1 lb (375–500 g) each, cleaned, head and tail intact

1–2 tablespoons unsalted butter, melted

Salt and freshly ground pepper

3-inch (7.5 cm) chive lengths for garnish

SEA BASS WITH FENNEL AND PERNOD

1 sea bass or red snapper, about 3 lb (1.5 kg), cleaned, head and tail intact

3–4 tablespoons unsalted butter, melted

4 teaspoons minced fresh tarragon or 2 teaspoons dried

3 cloves garlic, minced

Salt and freshly ground pepper

3 large fennel bulbs, trimmed, cored, and thinly sliced lengthwise, with fronds reserved for garnish

⅓ cup (3 fl oz/80 ml) Pernod, or to taste

Lemon wedges for garnish

Preheat the oven to 450°F (230°C). Rinse the sea bass under cold running water and pat dry with paper towels. Make 3 deep diagonal slashes in one side of the fish. Coat the fish with 1–2 tablespoons of the melted butter and sprinkle inside and out with the tarragon, garlic, and salt and pepper.

Select a heavy roasting pan just large enough to hold the fish comfortably and coat the bottom with 1 tablespoon of the melted butter. Place the fish, cut side up, in the roasting pan. Arrange the fennel slices around the fish. Drizzle the fennel liberally with the remaining melted butter and season to taste with salt and pepper.

Roast until the fish flakes easily when the flesh in one of the slashes is prodded gently with a fork, about 20 minutes.

Transfer the fish to a warmed platter, surround with the fennel, and sprinkle with the Pernod. Serve hot, garnished with lemon wedges and fennel fronds.

MAKES 6 SERVINGS

PERNOD

Pernod is a brand of anise-flavored liqueur that nicely accents the slight licorice flavor of the fennel in this dish. It is popular in France, where it is often mixed with water and served as an aperitif. As a cooking ingredient, Pernod especially complements seafood. You can substitute any anise-flavored liqueur such as anisette or pastis.

HALIBUT STEAKS AU POIVRE

Preheat the oven to 400°F (200°C). Rinse the halibut steaks under cold running water and pat dry with paper towels. Brush the fish with enough of the melted butter to coat well. Sprinkle with the pepper and press gently so the pepper adheres to the fish. Put the tomatoes and basil leaves in a buttered roasting pan just large enough to hold the fish comfortably, and arrange the fish on top of the tomatoes.

Roast until the halibut flakes easily when gently prodded with a fork, 8–10 minutes.

Using a spatula, transfer the halibut steaks and tomatoes to warmed individual plates and serve hot.

Serving Tip: Serve with buttered spinach fettuccine or whole-wheat (wholemeal) fettuccine.

MAKES 6 SERVINGS

6 halibut steaks, each about ¾ inch (2 cm) thick

2–3 tablespoons unsalted butter, melted

1 teaspoon black peppercorns, crushed, or to taste

2 large tomatoes, sliced

¼ cup (¼ oz/7 g) fresh basil leaves

PEPPERCORNS

For the best flavor, always grind or crush pepper just before using it. For this dish, crush whole black peppercorns in a mortar with a pestle. To give the steaks a colorful look and an interesting change in flavor, use a blend of black, green, and white—or even pink—peppercorns. Black peppercorns are the hottest of the four. Green peppercorns are immature black peppercorns that have been brined to preserve them, and white peppercorns are black ones with the outer layer removed. Pink peppercorns are actually the berry of a type of rose plant.

BLUEFISH WITH TOMATO BUTTER

FOR THE TOMATO BUTTER:

3 shallots, minced

1 tablespoon tomato paste

¾ cup (6 oz/185 g) unsalted butter, cut into 1-inch (2.5-cm) pieces, at room temperature

6 bluefish or mackerel fillets, about 6 oz (185 g) each

1½–2 tablespoons olive oil

¼ cup (2 fl oz/60 ml) fresh lemon juice

2 teaspoons minced fresh oregano, plus sprigs for garnish

Salt and freshly ground pepper

To make the tomato butter, in a food processor, combine the shallots, tomato paste, and butter pieces and process until combined. Spoon the flavored butter into a small bowl, cover, and set aside.

Preheat the oven to 400°F (200°C). Rinse the bluefish under cold running water and pat dry with paper towels. Choose a roasting pan just large enough to hold the fish comfortably. Coat the pan with 1 tablespoon of the olive oil and put the fish in the pan. Brush the fish liberally with the remaining oil. Sprinkle evenly with the lemon juice, oregano, and salt and pepper to taste.

Roast until the fish flakes easily when prodded gently with a fork, 8–10 minutes.

Arrange the fish on warmed individual plates, garnish with oregano sprigs and a pat of tomato butter, and serve hot.

Serving Tip: Accompany the fish with roasted cherry tomatoes (page 91).

MAKES 6 SERVINGS

BLUEFISH

The feisty bluefish, found along the coast of Maine, earns its nickname "bulldog of the ocean" by chasing mackerel right up onto the beach. Bluefish have a soft flesh and delicate yet distinctive flavor. They range from 3 to 10 pounds (1.5 to 5 kg), and their dark, oily flesh lightens as it cooks. Mackerel is a good substitute.

VEGETABLES AND FRUITS

Roasting has a wonderful effect on vegetables. When brushed with butter or oil and slipped into the oven, green beans and asparagus become tender and sweet. In the case of roasted fruits such as apples and plums, the contrast of caramelized exteriors with soft interiors illustrates irresistibly how roasting can bring out the best of sweet as well as savory ingredients.

ASPARAGUS WITH PROSCIUTTO

Preheat the oven to 400°F (200°C). Arrange the asparagus spears in an oiled shallow roasting pan just large enough to hold them comfortably. Drizzle the asparagus with olive oil and turn the spears to coat. Wrap each spear with prosciutto and then sprinkle with pepper to taste.

Roast the asparagus, turning once with tongs, until the spears are tender-crisp, about 15 minutes.

Arrange the asparagus on a warmed platter and sprinkle with the lemon zest. Serve hot or warm.

MAKES 6 SERVINGS

18–20 thick asparagus spears, trimmed and peeled (far left)

Extra-virgin olive oil for coating

9–10 paper-thin slices prosciutto, cut in half lengthwise

Freshly ground pepper

1 tablespoon grated lemon zest

PREPARING ASPARAGUS

Roasting is an excellent way to bring out the delicious, unique flavor of asparagus. To trim asparagus, gently bend the spears near the bottom until the woody part snaps off. For thick spears, peel with a vegetable peeler to within 2 inches (5 cm) of the tops. This will help them cook through evenly and make them more tender.

ROASTED CHERRY TOMATOES

1½ lb (750 g) cherry
tomatoes

1 cup (2 oz/60 g) fresh
whole-wheat (wholemeal)
bread crumbs (page 70)

1 tablespoon thinly sliced
fresh basil leaves, plus
whole leaves for garnish

2 cloves garlic, minced

Salt and freshly ground
pepper

½ lb (250 g) fresh mozzarella
cheese, preferably buffalo
mozzarella *(far right),*
drained and cut into
¼-inch (6-mm) slices

Preheat the oven to 400°F (200°C). Select a roasting pan just large enough to hold the tomatoes comfortably. Line the pan with aluminum foil, then oil the foil.

Cut the tomatoes in half and layer them, cut side up, in the prepared pan. In a small bowl, combine the bread crumbs, sliced basil, garlic, and salt and pepper to taste. Sprinkle the crumb mixture over the tomatoes.

Roast the tomatoes until they are soft and beginning to shrivel around the edges, about 15 minutes. Transfer the tomatoes to a warmed platter or shallow bowl and arrange the cheese slices around them. Garnish with basil leaves and serve.

MAKES 6 SERVINGS

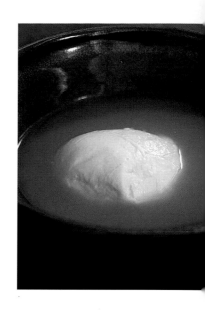

BUFFALO MOZZARELLA

In Italy, mozzarella is
traditionally made from
the milk of water buffaloes.
Cow's milk mozzarella is
more common elsewhere,
however, and is widespread
in Italy as well. Fresh buffalo
mozzarella has a tangier
flavor than its cow's milk
counterpart, and it is also
pricier. If you can find it,
try it in this recipe. Fresh
mozzarella is highly
perishable. Store it in its
liquid on the bottom shelf
of the refrigerator, and
serve it within a day or
two of purchase.

GREEN BEANS AND ONIONS

Preheat the oven to 425°F (220°C). Bring a large saucepan three-fourths full of water to a boil. Add a pinch of salt and the green beans. Cook the beans until they turn bright green and are just tender, 1–2 minutes. The timing will depend on the age and size of the beans. Drain the beans and plunge them into a bowl of ice-cold water to stop the cooking. Drain and set aside.

Combine the onion and tomatoes in a heavy baking dish. Add the green beans, oregano, and salt and pepper to taste. Drizzle the olive oil over the vegetables and toss to coat.

Cover with aluminum foil and roast until the beans are tender-crisp, about 20 minutes. Uncover the dish and continue roasting until just tender, 15–20 minutes longer (for a total roasting time of 35–40 minutes). Stir the beans 3 or 4 times during roasting. Taste and adjust the seasoning.

Transfer the bean mixture to a serving bowl or platter and serve hot or at room temperature, with tzatziki spooned over the top, if desired.

Variation Tip: Instead of serving this dish with tzatziki, sprinkle the green beans and onions with capers.

MAKES 6–8 SERVINGS

TZATZIKI

This garlicky Greek yogurt-cucumber sauce is a zesty complement to mild green beans and may also be used as a dip for pita bread or a topping for kabobs. Lightly salt and drain 1 cup (5 oz/ 155 g) peeled, seeded, finely chopped cucumber in a colander for 30 minutes. In a bowl, mix together the drained cucumber, 1 cup (8 oz/250 g) plain yogurt, and 2 teaspoons minced garlic. For a thicker sauce, drain the yogurt in a colander lined with a double layer of cheesecloth (muslin) for at least 3 hours or up to overnight in the refrigerator.

Salt and freshly ground pepper

2 lb (1 kg) fresh green beans, trimmed

1 large white onion, chopped

3 large tomatoes, chopped

4 teaspoons minced fresh oregano or 2 teaspoons dried

¼ cup (2 fl oz/60 ml) extra-virgin olive oil

Tzatziki for serving (*far left*) (optional)

ROASTED RADICCHIO AND ENDIVE

3 heads Verona radicchio,
halved lengthwise

3 Belgian endives, halved
lengthwise

6 tablespoons (3 oz/90 g)
unsalted butter, melted

Salt and freshly ground
pepper

2 tablespoons finely
chopped fresh chives,
plus extra for garnish

½ cup (2½ oz/75 g)
crumbled fresh goat
cheese

Place an oven rack in the lower third of the oven and preheat the oven to 400°F (200°C). Arrange the radicchio and endives in a roasting pan just large enough to hold them comfortably in a single layer. Pour the melted butter over the leaves and turn to coat. Season with salt and pepper to taste and sprinkle with the 2 tablespoons chives.

Roast the radicchio and endives for 10 minutes. Remove the pan from the oven and, using 2 spoons, turn the greens over. Return the pan to the oven and continue roasting until tender, about 10 minutes longer, for a total roasting time of 20 minutes.

Arrange 1 radicchio half and 1 endive half on each plate, sprinkle with the goat cheese, and garnish with chives. Serve at once.

MAKES 6 SERVINGS

THE CHICORY FAMILY
Radicchio and Belgian endive are both types of chicory, a family of bitter greens. Two types of radicchio are now typically available. Round *radicchio di Verona,* with reddish purple leaves on creamy white stems, is the most common, while *radicchio di Treviso* has long, narrow mostly green leaves with red tips. Belgian endive is carefully cultivated to produce small, narrow white leaves tipped with yellow or sometimes rose. Roasting nicely mellows the bitterness of the greens. Radicchio and endive are both at their best in autumn and winter, when cool weather brings out their sweetness.

ROASTED BEETS
WITH BALSAMIC-DRESSED GREENS

PREPARING BEETS

Roasting beets is a great way to enhance their sweetness without leaching out flavor and color. Leaving 1 inch (2.5 cm) or so of the stems on the beets helps to keep them from bleeding juice. When slicing cooked beets, be aware that they will stain anything they touch—cutting boards, clothes, fingertips—a bright red. Beet greens are highly nutritious, providing calcium, potassium, vitamin C, vitamin A, and folate.

Preheat the oven to 400°F (200°C). Remove the green tops from the beets, leaving about 1 inch (2.5 cm) of the stems and the tails intact. Rinse and reserve the green tops. Scrub the beets, being careful not to break the skin. Coat the beets with olive oil, then wrap in aluminum foil and arrange them in a single layer in a roasting pan.

Roast the beets until they can be pierced easily with a sharp knife, about 1 hour, depending on the size of the beets.

Meanwhile, prepare the beet greens. Using a small, sharp knife, cut off and discard any thick stems. Bring a saucepan three-fourths full of water to a boil and add a pinch of salt and the greens. Boil just until wilted, about 30 seconds. Drain and let cool. Shred the greens and place in a bowl. Toss with the vinegar, the 3 tablespoons olive oil, and salt and pepper to taste.

Remove the beets from the oven and let cool. Peel the beets and cut them into slices about ¼ inch (6 mm) thick. Place the beets in a bowl and toss with the sliced onion. Season to taste with salt and pepper. Serve at room temperature, surrounded by the greens. Pass the sour cream at the table.

Serving Tip: This dish is excellent served alongside roasted garlic mashed potatoes.

MAKES 6 SIDE-DISH SERVINGS

2 bunches medium beets, including green tops

3 tablespoons extra-virgin olive oil, plus extra for coating

Salt and freshly ground pepper

3 tablespoons balsamic vinegar

1 large red onion, sliced

1 cup (8 oz/250 g) sour cream

ROASTED AUTUMN VEGETABLES

8 tablespoons (4 oz/125 g) unsalted butter, melted

2 large sweet potatoes or yams, scrubbed, peeled, and cut into rounds ½ inch (12 mm) thick

4 large carrots, peeled and thickly sliced on the diagonal

4 large parsnips, peeled and cut into rounds ½ inch (12 mm) thick

3 tablespoons wildflower honey

Salt and freshly ground pepper

3 tablespoons fresh lemon juice

½ cup (3 oz/90 g) golden raisins (sultanas)

Preheat the oven to 425°F (220°C). Using 2 tablespoons of the melted butter, grease a roasting pan just large enough to hold the vegetables comfortably. Arrange the sweet potatoes, carrots, and parsnips in the prepared pan. Toss the vegetables with the remaining 6 tablespoons (3 fl oz/90 ml) melted butter, then drizzle them with the honey. Sprinkle with salt and pepper to taste, the lemon juice, and the raisins.

Roast the vegetables, turning twice, until tender, about 1 hour.

Using 2 large spoons, gently transfer the vegetables to a warmed platter. Serve hot.

Serving Tip: If desired, before serving the roasted vegetables, stir them with a wooden spoon to break them up and mash them together for a homey, comforting side dish.

MAKES 8 SERVINGS

PARSNIPS

The first frost turns parsnips sweet, so this creamy-colored root vegetable is at its best in late autumn and early winter. It is excellent for roasting. Add parsnips to the pan alongside other root vegetables when you roast meats and poultry. To prepare parsnips (and other root vegetables), peel with a vegetable peeler, then cut into thick slices. Like potatoes, parsnips will start to discolor after they are sliced unless they are sprinkled with an acidic ingredient such as lemon juice.

ROASTED-APPLE BROWN BETTY

Preheat the oven to 400°F (200°C). Toss the apples with the granulated sugar, cinnamon, and nutmeg. Mound the apples in a roasting pan just large enough to hold them comfortably.

Roast, turning twice, until fork-tender, about 1 hour. Drain the apples, reserving the liquid. Let cool. In a food processor, purée the apples, adding the reserved liquid as needed to make a thick applesauce.

Reduce the oven temperature to 375°F (190°C). Toss the bread crumbs with the melted butter. Sprinkle half of the crumbs over the bottom of an 8-inch (20-cm) round or square baking pan. Pour the applesauce over the crumbs and sprinkle the remaining crumbs on top. Bake for 20 minutes.

To serve, spoon into shallow bowls and top with the hard sauce.

MAKES 6–8 SERVINGS

HARD SAUCE

The traditional accompaniment to plum pudding, hard sauce pairs well with any hearty autumn or winter dessert. To make hard sauce, combine ½ cup (4 oz/125 g) unsalted butter at room temperature, 1 cup (2 oz/60 g) sifted confectioners' (icing) sugar, 1 tablespoon dark rum or brandy or 1 teaspoon vanilla extract (essence), and ⅛ teaspoon freshly grated nutmeg. Mix well to blend. If desired, chill before serving.

2½ lb (1.25 kg) Golden Delicious or Granny Smith apples, peeled, cored, and cut into slices ¼ inch (6 mm) thick

¾ cup (6 oz/185 g) granulated sugar

1 teaspoon ground cinnamon

¼ teaspoon freshly grated nutmeg

2 cups (8 oz/250 g) dried white bread crumbs (page 70) or graham cracker crumbs

4 tablespoons (2 oz/60 g) unsalted butter, melted

Hard sauce *(far left)*, vanilla ice cream, or sweetened whipped cream for serving

PLUMS WITH CANDIED GINGER

2 lb (1 kg) ripe dark purple plums, pitted and quartered

⅓ cup (2 oz/60 g) candied ginger *(far right),* finely chopped

½ cup (1½ oz/45 g) old-fashioned rolled oats

½ cup (4 oz/125 g) sugar

6 tablespoons (3 oz/90 g) unsalted butter, at room temperature

¼ cup (1½ oz/45 g) all-purpose (plain) flour

Vanilla ice cream for serving

Preheat the oven to 400°F (200°C). Put the plums in a buttered shallow 8-inch (20-cm) square baking pan just large enough to hold them comfortably. Toss the plums with the candied ginger. Set aside.

In a food processor, combine the oats, sugar, butter, and flour. Pulse for a few seconds until coarsely chopped. The mixture will clump together. Sprinkle the oat mixture evenly over the plums.

Roast until the plums are bubbling and the top is browned, about 30 minutes.

Scoop the ice cream into dessert bowls and spoon the warm plums on top.

MAKES 6–8 SERVINGS

CANDIED GINGER

You can buy candied, or crystallized, ginger at the supermarket—or make it yourself at home. For home-made, bring 1½ cups (12 fl oz/375 ml) water to a boil. Stir in ½ cup (4 oz/125 g) sugar until dissolved. Cook over medium heat for 5 minutes, then add 1 cup (4 oz/125 g) thinly sliced (⅛ inch/3 mm) peeled fresh ginger. Reduce the heat to a simmer and cook until tender, about 10 minutes. Drain, then put the ginger in a bowl with ½ cup (4 oz/125 g) sugar and toss to coat. Spread out in a single layer and let cool. Store in a tightly covered jar for up to 3 weeks.

ROASTING BASICS

Roasting need not be limited to a turkey or beef for a holiday dinner. Many other foods can also be roasted, including a wide variety of meats, poultry, fish and shellfish, and a number of fruits and vegetables. And because preparations for roasting are minimal—trussing, trimming, seasoning, stuffing, marinating—once the food is in the oven, your work is almost done. The resulting rich brown crusts and tender interiors will inspire you to enjoy roasting year-round.

ROASTING

Roasting is one of the oldest and simplest forms of cooking. Although it stems from the ancient practice of cooking food on a spit over an open fire, today the term "roasting" refers to cooking food in an uncovered pan in the dry heat of an oven.

Roasting works well for tender cuts of meat with plenty of marbled interior fat, for poultry with the skin on, or for seafood, which is lean but cooks quickly enough that it will not dry out in the oven. Tougher cuts of meat like the shoulder or flank are better reserved for cooking methods that depend on added moisture, such as stewing and braising. Some vegetables and fruits—potatoes and other root vegetables, apples, pears—also take well to roasting.

One of the most appealing qualities of roasted foods is the beautiful and delicious brown crusts that develop in the oven. Contact with heat causes the sugars and proteins in food to form compounds on the surface similar to caramel, forming a flavorful crust. Simultaneously, the steady oven heat slowly penetrates to the center of the food, which remains juicy. This irresistible counterpoint of caramelized crust and tender interior makes roasting a favorite cooking method.

EQUIPMENT

A roasting pan is indispensable for cooking large cuts of meat and poultry. Its low sides allow the oven heat to reach as much of the surface of the food as possible, while catching juices that drip during roasting. Choose a heavy stainless steel, aluminum, or enameled steel roasting pan to ensure even heat and to keep the bottom of the food and the pan drippings from burning. Although a nonstick pan makes cleanup easy, a regular surface allows more bits to adhere to the pan and brown during roasting, contributing later to a delicious pan sauce or gravy. Many other kinds of cookware may also be used for roasting, including glass, ovenproof porcelain, or earthenware dishes, and even rimmed baking sheets. Choose a pan or dish that holds the food comfortably, leaving enough room for the oven heat to circulate freely around the food and so that you can spoon up or siphon juices for basting. If you are using a nonmetal pan for roasting, and the recipe calls for transferring the pan to the stove top for sauce making, you will need to make sure it is flameproof.

Placing food to be roasted on a metal roasting rack keeps the bottom of the food from stewing in the pan drippings and sticking to the pan. It also helps to produce clearer pan drippings, which means better-tasting sauces and gravies. You can use an inverted pie pan to prop up a roast in a pinch, but a V-shaped roasting rack, which both elevates the food and allows more of its surface to brown, is best. A rack will also make removing the roasted food from the pan easier. If you don't use a rack, shift the meat or chicken after about 20 minutes of roasting to loosen it from the pan.

PREPARING TO ROAST

Most of the work in roasting takes place before the actual cooking. Meat and poultry often need to be trimmed or trussed, and you will want to add flavor with herbs, spices, and other ingredients. But once the food is in the oven, you need only baste (or sometimes turn) the food occasionally, leaving you free to tend to other tasks or to spend time with guests, while enjoying the savory aromas and awaiting the tender results.

RINSING

Since unpleasant or even dangerous bacteria live on the surface of meat, poultry, and seafood, it is a good idea to rinse these foods before roasting. Remove the giblets from the cavity of whole poultry first. Rinse the meat, poultry, or seafood under cold running water (for whole poultry or fish, rinse out the cavity as well), then pat dry with paper towels.

TRIMMING

Meats such as chops and roasts are usually already trimmed closely of fat, but you may need to trim them more. Fat renders off during cooking and may burn, while the membranes will shrink and cause meats to curl up. Trim the fat to a ⅛-inch (3-mm) layer, and use the tip of a sharp knife to slit membranes at 1-inch (2.5-cm) intervals around the meat.

TRUSSING

Although it's not essential, trussing poultry gives it a nicer shape and helps keep the drumstick and wing tips from overbrowning. Use sturdy linen kitchen string, if possible, as it is less likely than cotton string to scorch in the oven. To truss a whole bird, set it breast side up on a work surface. Tuck each wing tip under the second joint of the wing to keep it in place, then tuck the wings as much as possible under the body. (You should do this even if you don't plan to truss the rest of the bird.) To secure the drumsticks, cut a piece of string 12–14 inches (30–35 cm) long. Place the bird in a roasting pan and cross the drumsticks. Wind the string around the drumsticks and tie the ends together tightly.

For longer-cooking birds such as a whole turkey, pull the skin from the breast over the neck opening and secure it in place with a needle and thread, toothpicks, or small metal poultry skewers. This helps keep the bird moist.

Whole fillets of beef, pork, or lamb roast more evenly when trussed. Boneless roasts are also tied to give them a more uniform, attractive shape and to make them easier to carve. Usually the butcher will already have tied the roast before purchase. If not, fold any thin ends under the roast and secure them with kitchen string. Continue tying the string around the roast at 2- to 3-inch (5- to 7.5-cm) intervals.

Fish fillets do not need to be tied, but you should tuck the thin end under the rest of the fillet to keep it from drying out before the whole piece is cooked through.

ADDING FLAVOR

Marinating is the most common way to flavor a roast. Seasoning blends, known as rubs or dry marinades, are rubbed directly onto the surface of food. Wet marinades add moisture as well as flavor, and can help tenderize meat or poultry when they include an acidic liquid such as wine or citrus juice (see page 54).

For convenience, put the marinade and the food in a large zippered plastic freezer bag. Press out the air, seal, place in a bowl (in case of leaks), and refrigerate. Turn the bag occasionally to guarantee even marinating.

The skin of poultry may also be loosened starting at the neck, and fresh herbs such as sage or basil leaves slipped under the skin over the breast to add flavor. Herb sprigs, lemons, onions, and other vegetables may also be placed in the cavities of poultry. Inserting slivers of garlic into meat before roasting is another way of adding flavor.

BARDING

Tying bacon slices or thin sheets of pork fat on top of a roast, a technique called barding, helps keep lean cuts of meat and the lean breast meat of poultry from drying out during roasting. After cooking, the fat is removed and usually discarded.

STUFFING

Mixtures of torn bread, bread or cracker crumbs, grains, dried or fresh fruit, nuts, ground meat, and many other ingredients can be used to stuff the cavities of poultry or to layer between thin pieces of meat, poultry, or vegetables. Although it was long believed that stuffing helped to flavor roasted poultry and meat, the stuffing is actually the main flavor beneficiary. It absorbs juices from the roasted food, resulting in more moistness and flavor than stuffing baked separately.

BASTING

One of the most important tasks to remember when roasting is to baste regularly. While the food is roasting, pull out the oven rack and brush or spoon pan drippings, a marinade, or a glaze over the food. This adds color, promotes the formation of a crust, and slows the process of the food drying out during roasting.

Basting liquids are often the accumulated pan juices, but they can also be melted butter, flavored or not, or various mixtures based on water, stock, wine, or beer. These all add flavor, and those that contain sugar or protein—in the form of butter, corn syrup, honey, preserves, stock or broth, wine, or beer—promote even browning. Too much sugar can cause scorching, however, so don't go overboard. Basting liquids should also include fat, which enhances flavor.

If you are basting with a leftover meat or poultry marinade, stop using it at least 10 minutes before the end of cooking, to allow enough time for the heat to kill any bacteria that have been reintroduced by dipping a brush used on raw meat back into the marinade. If you want to use a marinade as a sauce, first bring the marinade to a boil and cook for a full minute.

ROASTING TIMES

Generally, the longer the roasting time, the lower the oven temperature. Some larger pieces of food, such as whole poultry, start out roasting at a higher temperature to help their surface brown and caramelize, then finish roasting at a lower temperature.

Start with food as close as possible to room temperature. Remove the food from the refrigerator shortly before you're ready to turn on the oven for preheating. This takes off some of the chill, so the outside won't overcook before the center is done. In the interest of safety, however, it is best not to leave uncooked meat or poultry out for more than 2 hours, or less time in warm weather.

Larger roasts are best cooked at an oven temperature of 325°–350°F (165°–180°C) to help prevent the outside of the roast from overcooking before the center is done. If the roast isn't as brown as it should be when it is nearly done, raise the temperature to 400°F (200°C) for the last few minutes of cooking. Smaller roasts, including beef tenderloins, do best roasted quickly at high temperatures. They are in the oven for a shorter time and need the higher heat to brown.

Although it's usually best to use a whole bird for roasted poultry, you can also roast smaller pieces such as the breast or drumsticks. Even if you prefer to remove the skin before eating to reduce the fat content, leave the skin on during roasting. The fat from the skin will help baste the bird and keep it moist, and won't add much fat.

For turning foods, use tongs or, for smaller foods, a large spoon. Avoid using a fork to turn foods; it will pierce the skin, allowing juices to run out. Turning a turkey requires caution. Remove the pan from the oven and carefully turn the bird over, gripping it with kitchen towels to keep the turkey from slipping.

DONENESS

Although marinating, coating with oil or butter, and basting will help keep the surface of roasted food moist, nothing will keep the center moist if you overcook it.

There are some sensory cues to use when testing roasted foods for doneness. Whole roast poultry is traditionally tested by piercing a thigh to see if the juices run clear with no trace of pink or red. With experience, you can assess the degree of doneness of meat by pressing it with your fingertip and noting the resistance you feel. The more resistance, the more well done the meat is.

However, the best way to judge a roast's internal temperature accurately is with an instant-read thermometer, a utensil widely available in cookware stores. At the earliest possible time the roast might be done, insert the thermometer into the thickest part, making sure that it does not touch bone. (Bone conducts heat and will skew the reading.) For poultry, the thermometer should be inserted into the thickest part of the thigh. Within a few seconds or so, the thermometer will register the temperature. If further roasting is required, remove the thermometer and check again in 5–15 minutes; the timing will depend on how much higher the food's internal temperature has to rise.

Doneness temperatures will differ somewhat for different foods. The United States Food Safety and Inspection Service suggests a minimum temperature of 160°F (71°C) for cooked meat and poultry. This is the temperature needed to destroy all harmful bacteria. If you are pregnant, older, have a compromised immune system, are cooking for older people or young children, or want to limit your exposure to bacterial risk, you may want to observe this rule. Many people choose to cook meat to a lower temperature for juicier flesh and fuller flavor, however. The temperatures below are good guidelines.

MEAT

To judge the doneness of roasted meat with an instant-read thermometer, keep the following temperatures in mind. For beef, look for 125°F (52°C) for rare and 130°F (54°C) for medium-rare. Cooking beef beyond medium will cause it to dry out and become tough. Pork should reach 155°–160°F (68°–71°C). When roasting lamb, 125°F (52°C) indicates rosy-rare and 130°F (54°C) indicates medium-rare. For venison, look for 125°F (52°C) for rare. When roasting lamb and venison, do not cook them past the medium-rare stage, or you will end up with meat that is dry and stringy. Ground meats are more susceptible to contamination because most bacteria live on the meat's surface, and grinding mixes those bacteria throughout the meat. For safety, ground meats should be cooked to 160°F (71°C).

POULTRY

For roasted chicken, allow the temperature in the thickest part of the thigh to reach 170°F (77°C). Turkey breasts should register 165°F (74°C), and turkey thighs should be 180°F (82°C). For duck, allow the temperature to reach 180°F (82°C) in the thickest part of the thigh. When roasting goose, the breast should register 175°–180°F (80°–82°C).

FISH

Fish is done when its flesh firms up and turns opaque. Gently prod or cut into the top of the fish with a knife tip or fork. The flaky sections should easily separate, but the flesh should still look moist. An old rule of thumb calls for cooking fish for 10 minutes per inch. Keep in mind that it is easy to overcook fish, and start checking for doneness at the earliest opportunity.

RESTING

Keep in mind that the internal temperature of roasted food will continue to rise by 5°–10°F (2°–4°C) after it has been removed from the oven.

Before carving, a meat or poultry roast benefits from resting at room temperature for 5–15 minutes after it leaves the oven. This allows its juices time to settle back into the meat and permits the internal temperature to stabilize. Tenting a finished roast with aluminum foil will keep it warm while it rests, but note that this will cause the skin to steam slightly.

CARVING

A two-pronged fork to steady the roast and a good-quality sharp knife make carving easier. An all-purpose slicing knife may be used for carving any type of roast, but certain knives are better suited to some roasts than others. A knife with a long, flexible, but sturdy blade is best for following the contours of a large turkey. A shorter, sturdier knife makes quick work of the smaller chicken. Long, straight blades with serrated edges or ovate indentations cut more readily through red meats and ham. Whatever knife you use, make sure it is very sharp for easier, safer carving. A sturdy, slip-resistant carving board, preferably with a narrow groove around the perimeter to capture escaping juices, helps keep the meat firmly in place.

To carve a whole roasted chicken, first remove the wings. Cut through the skin between the wing and breast. Pull the wing away from the body to locate the shoulder joint. Cut through the joint to remove the wing.

Next, remove the legs. Set the chicken breast side up and cut through the skin between the thigh and breast. Pull the leg away from the body to locate the thigh joint. Cut through the joint to remove the entire leg. Then cut through the knee joint to separate the leg and thigh.

Now, carve the breast. Just above the thigh and wing joints, make a deep horizontal cut through the breast toward the bone to create a base cut. Starting near the breastbone, carve thin slices vertically, cutting downward to end each slice at the base cut. Angle the knife as you near the bone.

The steps for carving a larger bird such as a turkey are similar, but you will want to cut through the joint separating the drumstick and the thigh. Carve both of these pieces, cutting the meat in slices parallel to the bone.

When carving meat, for the best results always carve across the grain—perpendicular, not parallel, to its fibers. Use the carving fork to steady the meat and cut crosswise into thick slices with the knife. This produces a more handsome slice and avoids long strands of tough meat. The leaner the meat to be carved, the thinner the slice should be for ease of chewing. Do not change the direction of the knife blade in midslice, or the pieces will be ragged and uneven.

DEGLAZING

This technique is used to make sauces and gravies. First, liquid is added to the hot pan to dislodge the browned bits of meat or poultry that become stuck to the pan bottom during roasting. Remove the roast from the pan, pour off excess fat, and set the pan on a burner. Pour in wine, stock, or water. Heat the liquid over medium-high, stirring and scraping the pan bottom with a wooden spoon to loosen the browned bits. Before long, the liquid will partly evaporate, leaving behind juices with a more concentrated flavor. The result is often called a reduction sauce or pan sauce, and is delicious on its own or as a base for other sauces such as gravy (page 110).

BASIC RECIPES

CHICKEN STOCK

4 lb (2 kg) chicken bones, or 1 chicken, 3–4 lb (1.5–2 kg), plus 1 lb (500 g) chicken wings and necks

1 large yellow onion, quartered

4 carrots, quartered

3 celery stalks, including leaves, cut into 1-inch (2.5-cm) pieces

6 fresh flat-leaf (Italian) parsley sprigs

1 tablespoon fresh tarragon leaves

6 peppercorns

2 bay leaves

2 teaspoons salt

3 qt (3 l) water

Place the chicken bones or chicken in a large stockpot. Add the onion, carrots, celery, parsley, tarragon, peppercorns, bay leaves, salt, and water. Bring to a boil over high heat, skimming the surface to remove any foam. Cover partially, reduce the heat to low, and simmer gently for 3½–4 hours. Skim occasionally to remove any foam.

Strain the stock through a sieve lined with a double layer of cheesecloth (muslin). Discard the solids (or use the meat to make another dish). Let cool, cover, and refrigerate overnight. Remove any hardened fat from the surface of the stock.

Refrigerate the stock if you intend to use it within a few days; if not, pour it into small covered containers and freeze until needed. It will keep for up to 1 month. Makes about 2 qt (2 l).

ROASTED BEEF STOCK

2 lb (1 kg) beef short ribs

1 lb (500 g) beef marrow bones

1 large yellow onion, quartered

4 carrots, quartered

2 celery stalks, including leaves, cut into 1-inch (2.5-cm) pieces

2 cloves garlic

6 fresh flat-leaf (Italian) parsley sprigs

8 peppercorns

2 bay leaves

2 teaspoons salt

3 qt (3 l) water

Preheat the oven to 425°F (220°C). Arrange the ribs, bones, onion, carrots, celery, and garlic in a roasting pan. Roast for 45 minutes, stirring once.

Drain off the fat and put the ribs, bones, and vegetables in a large stockpot. Add the parsley, peppercorns, bay leaves, salt, and water. Bring to a boil over high heat, skimming the surface to remove any foam. Cover partially, reduce the heat to low, and simmer gently for 3½–4 hours. Skim occasionally to remove any foam.

Discard the meat and bones. Strain the stock through a sieve lined with a double layer of cheesecloth (muslin). Let cool, cover, and refrigerate overnight. Remove any hardened fat from the surface.

Refrigerate the stock if you intend to use it within a few days; if not, pour it into small covered containers and freeze until needed. It will keep for up to 1 month. Makes about 2 qt (2 l).

BASIC GRAVY

Some recipes in this book that will yield good drippings and pan juices for basic gravy are Turkey with Currant Glaze (page 17), Chicken with Lemon and Onion (page 26), Goose with Roasted Apples (page 38), or Standing Rib Roast (page 45). Shown opposite are the basic steps in making gravy.

1 Pouring off the fat: While the roast rests before carving, carefully pour off all but 3–5 tablespoons (1½–2½ fl oz/45–75 ml) of the drippings (fat and other pan juices) from the roasting pan.

2 Whisking in flour: Place the roasting pan with the reserved drippings on the stove top over medium heat. Whisk in 1–2 tablespoons flour and stir rapidly to incorporate the flour into the drippings and to break up any lumps. Cook briefly, stirring, until lightly browned.

3 Adding the stock: Raise the heat to high and pour in 1–2 cups (8–16 fl oz/250–500 ml) beef or chicken stock. Bring to a boil and deglaze the pan, stirring to remove the browned bits from the bottom of the pan. Reduce the heat to medium and simmer, stirring often, until the gravy is slightly thickened and no raw flour flavor remains, about 5 minutes. Stir in more stock if needed to achieve a saucelike consistency.

4 Straining the gravy: Season with salt and pepper. Pour through a fine-mesh sieve into a warmed gravy boat and stir in 1 tablespoon minced fresh herbs, if desired. Makes about 1¾ cups (14 fl oz/440 ml).

GLOSSARY

ARUGULA The leaves of this dark green plant, also called rocket, resemble deeply notched, elongated oak leaves. They have a nutty, tangy, and slightly peppery flavor. The larger leaves may be more pungent than small ones.

BUTTER, UNSALTED Many cooks favor unsalted butter for two reasons. First, salt in butter can add to the total amount of salt in a recipe, which can interfere with the taste of the dish. Second, unsalted butter is likely to be fresher, since salt acts as a preservative and prolongs shelf life. If you cannot find unsalted butter, salted butter will work in most recipes, but taste and adjust other salt in the recipe as needed.

CAPON This plump chicken is a neutered male bird. Capons weigh 5–8 pounds (2.5–4 kg) and are meaty, juicy, and ideal for roasting.

CAVIAR In the strictest use of the term, caviar is the sieved and salted roe, or eggs, of sturgeon. The most sought-after caviar comes from three types of sturgeon that swim in the Caspian Sea: beluga, osetra, and sevruga. Also delicious is the small golden roe of whitefish or the larger juicy, coral-colored roe of salmon.

CHINESE FIVE-SPICE POWDER Five-spice powder is a common seasoning in the kitchens of southern China and of Vietnam, where it is often used to flavor poultry for roasting. Although it is readily available in well-stocked food stores, making your own results in a more flavorful blend. Using a coffee grinder or mortar and pestle, grind together 1 star anise pod, broken into segments; 2 teaspoons Sichuan peppercorns; ¼ teaspoon fennel seeds; and ¼ teaspoon whole cloves. Mix in ¼ teaspoon ground cinnamon. Store in an airtight container in a dark place for up to 6 months.

CILANTRO Also called fresh coriander and Chinese parsley, cilantro is an herb with a distinctive, assertive flavor. Some describe it as citrusy or minty; others find hints of sage and parsley. It is best used fresh, as it loses flavor when dried. Cilantro plays an important role in the cuisines of Mexico, the Caribbean, India, Egypt, Thailand, Vietnam, and China, and the southwestern United States.

CORNISH HEN A cross between a Cornish game cock and a white Plymouth Rock hen, this small bird weighs about 1½ pounds (750 g), making a generous serving for one person or a modest meal for two. Poussins, baby chickens that weigh about 1 pound (500 g) each, may be used instead of Cornish hens, but decrease the cooking time by a third.

CURRANTS, DRIED While fresh currants are berrylike fruits grown and used widely in Europe, dried currants are actually Zante grapes, tiny raisins with a distinctively tart-sweet flavor. If they are unavailable, substitute raisins.

DUCK The Long Island duckling, also known as a White Pekin duck, has mild, tender, relatively lean meat and is ideal for roasting whole. A duck has a heavier ratio of bone to flesh than a chicken does, so an average 5- to 6-pound (2.5- to 3-kg) duckling will yield only 3 or 4 servings.

EGGS, HARD-BOILED It's easy to over-cook hard-boiled eggs, giving their yolks an unsightly greenish tinge and a dry texture. This gentle method ensures good results: Put the eggs in a saucepan and add cold water to cover them by at least 1 inch (2.5 cm). Bring to a boil over medium heat. When the water begins to boil, remove from the heat, cover tightly, and let the eggs stand in the water for 20 minutes. Rinse under cold running water until cool, then peel.

GARLIC A pungent member of the onion family, garlic is fundamental to cuisines throughout the world. To peel garlic, crush a clove slightly with the flat side of a knife and remove the papery skin.

GIBLETS A term referring to the heart, gizzard, and liver of a turkey or other poultry. In a purchased bird, the giblets, along with the neck, are often placed in a small paper package and stuffed inside the cavity. If not used in a recipe, they may be discarded or put to another use—they make a nice addition to gravy and to dressing or stuffing.

GREEN ONIONS Also known as scallions or spring onions, green onions are the immature shoots of the bulb onion, with a narrow white base that has not yet begun to swell and long, hollow, flat green leaves. Green onions are mild in flavor and can be used chopped as a garnish.

HOISIN SAUCE A thick, sweet, dark brown Chinese sauce made from soybeans, sugar, garlic, five-spice powder or star anise, and a hint of chile. It can be thick and creamy or thin enough to pour. It is rubbed on meat and poultry before roasting to give them a sweet flavor. Hoisin sauce sometimes appears as a condiment, but it should be used judiciously, as its strong flavor can easily overpower most foods.

MUSHROOMS
Mushrooms absorb water readily, and will become soggy and flavorless if immersed for too long. To clean them, wipe with a damp cloth or brush. Special mushroom brushes are available for gentle removal of dirt. Following are some of the most popular varieties used in this cookbook.

Cremini: Common brown mushrooms, cremini are closely related to common white mushrooms and the two varieties are interchangeable. Cremini have a firm texture and full flavor. Large, fully mature cremini are known as portobello mushrooms. Some smaller cremini are now labeled Baby Bellas.

Morel: Considered the king of mushrooms, the morel has an intense, musky flavor that makes it highly prized. The uncultivated mushroom has a dark, elongated, spongelike cap and hollow stem. Unlike other mushrooms, morels should be immersed *briefly* in a large bowl of water to agitate and dislodge all the sand that tends to fill the crevices in their caps.

Oyster: Cream to pale gray in color, with a fan shape, oyster mushrooms have a subtle flavor similar to shellfish. They used to be found only as wild mushrooms but are now cultivated.

Porcino: Also called ceps, porcino mushrooms are pale brown, smooth, and have a woodsy flavor. In the United States, porcini are most commonly available dried, although fresh mushrooms can be found in autumn.

Shiitake: Meaty in flavor, these Asian mushrooms have flat, dark brown caps usually 2–3 inches (5–7.5 cm) wide and a rich, almost tealike flavor. They are available fresh or dried.

White: The cultivated, all-purpose mushroom, this variety is sold in grocery stores. They are sometimes called button mushrooms, although this term refers specifically to young, tender white mushrooms with closed caps.

MUSTARD, DIJON True Dijon mustard is made in Dijon, France, from dark brown mustard seeds (unless marked blanc), white wine or wine vinegar, and herbs. Silky smooth and fairly hot and sharp tasting, Dijon mustard and non-French blends labeled Dijon style are widely available in supermarkets.

NUTS
Almond: These delicate, fragrant nuts have a pointed, oval shape and a smooth texture that lends itself well to elegant presentations.

Pine: The seeds of certain pine species, pine nuts can be found nestled in the scales of pine cones. They are small and rich, with an elongated, slightly tapered shape and a resinous, sweet flavor.

NUTS, TOASTING Toasting brings out the flavor of nuts, turns them a pale gold, and makes them nicely crunchy. To toast nuts, place a small amount in a dry frying pan on the stove top. Place over medium heat and toast, stirring frequently, until lightly golden, 5–10 minutes, depending on the size of the nuts. Do not allow them to darken too much. Immediately transfer to a plate and let cool completely before using. Nuts continue to color off the heat, so toast them a shade lighter than desired. Store toasted nuts in a closed container for 2–3 days at room temperature.

OLIVE OIL This oil is primarily made in Mediterranean countries, California, and

Australia from the fruit of the olive tree. The term "extra-virgin" refers to oil from the first pressing of the olives that has been produced without the use of heat or chemicals. Extra-virgin olive oil has low acidity, a clear green or brownish hue, and a fine, fruity, sometimes slightly peppery flavor. The highest-quality extra-virgin olive oils should be reserved for dressings and drizzling over finished dishes. Those olive oils labeled "mild," "light," "pure," or simply "olive oil" are more highly processed and have less fragrance and color than extra-virgin. These varieties are better suited for everyday cooking.

OYSTERS Always buy oysters from reputable merchants. Live oysters in the shell should have a mild, sweet smell. Their shells should be closed tightly and feel heavy. Do not buy oysters that remain open when touched. A strong fishy or ammonia odor indicates the oysters are no longer fresh, so pass them by.

To store live oysters, spread them in a container and cover with a damp cloth. If needed, keep them in the refrigerator for 1–2 days, making sure the cloth stays moist. They will die if submerged in tap water or sealed in an airtight container.

PORT This sweet wine, fortified with grape alcohol, is a specialty of Portugal, although it is also bottled elsewhere. Ports range in quality from complex vintage Ports to sweet ruby Ports. Tawny Port, blended from grapes from several vintages and aged in wood for up to

40 years, is a moderately priced choice that's good for both cooking and drinking.

SHERRY A specialty of southwestern Spain, sherry is a fortified wine. It is made from the Palomino Fino grape and comes in eight different types, distinguished primarily by color, flavor, sweetness, and alcohol content. The best known of these are pale gold, dry fino; very pale, very dry manzanilla; darker, slightly nutty, and dry to medium-dry amontillado; and mahogany brown, highly aromatic, sweet cream sherry.

SHRIMP, DEVEINING Deveining, or removing the dark, visible intestinal tract that runs along the outer curve of a shrimp (prawn), is done primarily for aesthetic reasons when the "vein" is black and clearly visible. To devein a peeled, raw shrimp, use a small knife to cut a shallow groove along the back of the shrimp. With the tip of the knife, gently lift and scrape away the dark vein, then rinse the shrimp under cold running water. Drain the shrimp on paper towels and proceed with the recipe.

VENISON The lean meat of deer, venison has a dark red color, fine-grained dense texture, and robust flavor.

VINEGAR
Balsamic: Balsamic vinegar is a specialty of the Italian region of Emilia-Romagna, primarily the town of Modena. It is made from white Trebbiano grapes and is aged in wooden casks, which contributes to its

final flavor. Authentic balsamic vinegar is designated by the words *aceto balsamico tradizionale* and must be aged for at least 12 years (but often for much longer). This concentrated, syrupy liquid is prized for its rich, intense flavor and is used sparingly as a condiment and to flavor sauces. Younger balsamic vinegar, aged 1–3 years, is also available and is more appropriate for cooking. The commercial "balsamic vinegar" commonly found in supermarkets is either a blend of young balsamic vinegar and wine vinegar (this type, too, is made in Modena) or wine vinegar that is flavored with caramel. The better commercial vinegars are often very good and are fine for marinades, sauces, and salad dressings.

Cider: Made from apples, cider vinegar is commonly used in many traditional American recipes and is noted for its distinctive apple flavor. For the best flavor, buy real cider vinegar, not cider-flavored distilled vinegar.

Red Wine: Produced when wine is fermented for a second time, red wine vinegar is sharply acidic. The vinegar, like the wine from which it is made, has a more robust flavor than vinegar produced from white wine.

INDEX

SIMON & SCHUSTER SOURCE
A Division of Simon & Schuster, Inc.
Rockefeller Center
1230 Avenue of the Americas
New York, NY 10020

WILLIAMS-SONOMA
Founder and Vice-Chairman: Chuck Williams
Book Buyer: Cecilia Prentice

WELDON OWEN INC.
Chief Executive Officer: John Owen
President: Terry Newell
Chief Operating Officer: Larry Partington
Vice President, International Sales: Stuart Laurence
Creative Director: Gaye Allen
Series Editor: Sarah Putman Clegg
Associate Editor: Heather Belt
Art Director: Catherine Jacobes
Production Manager: Chris Hemesath
Shipping and Production Coordinator: Libby Temple

Weldon Owen wishes to thank the following
people for their generous assistance and support
in producing this book: Copy Editor Carolyn Miller;
Consulting Editor Sharon Silva; Designer
Douglas Chalk; Food Stylists Kim Konecny and
Erin Quon; Photographer's Assistant Faiza Ali;
Proofreaders Desne Ahlers, Carrie Bradley, and
Linda Bouchard; and Indexer Ken DellaPenta.

Williams-Sonoma Collection *Roasting* was
conceived and produced by Weldon Owen Inc.,
814 Montgomery Street, San Francisco,
California 94133, in collaboration with
Williams-Sonoma, 3250 Van Ness Avenue,
San Francisco, California 94109.

A Weldon Owen Production
Copyright © 2002 by Weldon Owen Inc. and
Williams-Sonoma Inc.

For information about special discounts for bulk
purchases, please contact Simon & Schuster
Special Sales: 1-800-456-6798 or
business@simonandschuster.com

Set in Trajan, Utopia, and Vectora.

Color separations by Bright Arts Graphics
Singapore (Pte.) Ltd.
Printed and bound in Singapore by Tien Wah Press
(Pte.) Ltd.

First printed in 2002.

10 9 8 7 6 5 4 3 2

Library of Congress Cataloging-in-Publication Data

Grunes, Barbara.
    Roasting / recipes and text, Barbara Grunes ;
general editor, Chuck Williams ; photographs,
Maren Caruso.
        p. cm. — (Williams-Sonoma collection)
    1. Roasting (Cookery) I. Title. II. Williams-
Sonoma collection (New York, N.Y.)

TX690 .G78 2002
641.7'1—dc21
                                    2002023033
ISBN 0-7432-2681-X

A NOTE ON WEIGHTS AND MEASURES

All recipes include customary U.S. and metric measurements. Metric conversions are based on
a standard developed for these books and have been rounded off. Actual weights may vary.